SKINNY COMFORT FOODS

SKINNY COOKING

Skinny Comfort

FOODS

◆————————◆

SUE SPITLER

SURREY BOOKS
CHICAGO

SKINNY COMFORT FOODS is published by Surrey Books, Inc.
230 E. Ohio St., Suite 120, Chicago, IL 60611.

First edition: 2 3 4 5

This book is manufactured in the United States of America.

Library of Congress Cataloging-in-Publication data:

Spitler, Sue.
    Skinny comfort foods / Sue Spitler.
    170p. cm.
    Includes index.
    ISBN 1-57284-006-4 (pbk.)
    1. Reducing diets—Recipes. 2. Cookery, American. I. Title.
RM222.S65 1996
641.5'637—dc20   96-24480
                                                                 CIP

Editorial and production: *Bookcrafters, Inc., Chicago*
Art Director: *Joan Sommers Design, Chicago*
Cover and interior illustrations by *Mona Daly*

For free catalog and prices on quantity purchases, contact Surrey Books at the
address above.

This title is distributed to the trade by Publishers Group West.

Titles in the "Skinny" Cookbooks Series:

Skinny Beef	*Skinny Pasta*
Skinny Chicken	*Skinny Pizzas*
Skinny Chocolate	*Skinny Potatoes*
Skinny Comfort Foods	*Skinny Sandwiches*
Skinny Desserts	*Skinny Sauces & Marinades*
Skinny Grilling	*Skinny Seafood*
Skinny Italian Cooking	*Skinny Soups*
Skinny Mexican Cooking	*Skinny Spices*
Skinny One-Pot Meals	*Skinny Vegetarian Entrées*

To my family and all the old-fashioned
comfort foods we remember.

Thank you, Pat Molden, for being my associate and collaborator
in this most enjoyable project. Also thank you's to publisher
Susan Schwartz and her staff for their support, and to Gene DeRoin,
editor, and Linda Yoakam, R.D., for their expert work behind
the scenes to produce this book of food memories.

CONTENTS

Introduction.. **xi**

1. SOUPS **1**

Cream of Tomato Soup, 2 Cream of Mushroom Soup, 3 Chicken
Noodle Soup, 4 Potato Chowder, 5 New England Clam Chowder, 6
Chili con Carne, 7 Navy Bean Soup with Ham, 9 Beef, Barley, and
Vegetable Soup, 10 Split Pea Soup with Ham, 11

2. MEATS.. **13**

Steak au Poivre, 14 Pepper Steak, 15 Chicken-Fried Steak, 16
Old-Fashioned Pot Roast, 17 Beef Bourguignonne, 19 Beef
Stroganoff, 20 Country Beef Stew, 21 Just Plain Meat Loaf, 22
Salisbury Steak with Mushroom Gravy, 23 Swedish Meatballs with
Noodles, 25 Roast Beef Hash, 26 Mock Chicken Legs, 27 Chop
Suey, 28 Shepherd's Pie, 29

3. POULTRY... **31**

Crisp Oven-Fried Chicken, 32 Roast Chicken with Cornbread
Stuffing, 33 Chicken Cordon Bleu, 34 Chicken à la King in Toast
Cups, 35 Chicken Paprikash, 37 Chicken Cacciatore, 38 Chicken
Stew with Parsley Dumplings, 39 Chicken Fricassee, 41 Glazed
Cornish Hens with Wild Rice, 42 Turkey Divan, 43 Turkey Pot Pie, 44

4. FISH **47**

Tuna Patties with Creamed Pea Sauce, 48 Poached Salmon with
Hollandaise Sauce, 50 Flounder en Papillote, 51 Shrimp De
Jonghe, 52 Seafood Newburg, 53

5. PASTA.. **55**

Macaroni and Cheese, 56 Turkey Tetrazzini, 57 Spaghetti and
Meatballs, 58 Linguine with White Clam Sauce, 60 Italian
Lasagne, 61

6. CHEESE AND EGGS... **63**

Eggs Benedict, 64 Quiche Lorraine, 65 Welsh Rarebit, 67 Cheddar
Cheese Soufflé, 68 Cheese Fondue, 69

7. VEGETABLES **71**
Artichokes with Hollandaise Sauce, 72 Green Bean Casserole, 73
New England Baked Beans, 74 Harvard Beets, 75 Cauliflower with
Creamy Cheese Sauce, 76 Corn Pudding, 77 Real Mashed Potatoes,
78 Potatoes Gratin, 79 Twice-Baked Potatoes with Cheese, 81
Crispy Fries, 82 Creamed Spinach, 83 Tomato Pudding, 84
Candied Yams, 86

8. SALADS **87**
Perfection Salad, 88 Frozen Fruit Salad, 89 Carrot-Raisin Salad, 90
Creamy Potato Salad, 91 German Potato Salad, 92 Macaroni Salad,
93 Freezer Coleslaw, 94 Waldorf Salad, 95 Wilted Spinach Salad,
96 Caesar Salad, 97 Ten-Layer Salad, 98

9. SANDWICHES **99**
Sloppy Joes, 100 Cheeseburgers Supreme, 101 Crab Melt, 102
Monte Cristo, 103

10. BREADS **105**
Garlic Bread, 106 Vinegar Biscuits, 107 Bubble Loaf, 108 English
Muffin Bread, 109 French Toast, 110 Banana Bread, 111 Sticky
Buns, 112

11. CAKES **115**
Sour Cream Coffee Cake with Apple-Date Filling, 116 Glazed
Orange Chiffon Cake, 118 Lemon Pound Cake, 119 Chocolate
Buttermilk Cake with Mocha Frosting, 121 Carrot Cake with Cream
Cheese Frosting, 123 Spice Cake with Penuche Frosting, 124
Pineapple Upside-Down Cake, 126 Boston Cream Pie, 127 Ice
Cream Jelly Roll Cake, 129

12. COOKIES **131**
Chocolate Chip Cookies, 132 Raisin Oatmeal Cookies, 133 Frosted
Sugar Cookies, 134 Tart Lemon Squares, 135 Frosted Cocoa
Brownies, 136

13. PIES AND PUDDINGS **137**
Grandma's Lemon Meringue Pie, 138 Banana Cream Pie, 140
Double Crust Apple Pie, 141 Spiced Sweet Potato Pie, 143
Angel Pie, 144 Raisin Bread Pudding, 145 Baked Cereal Pudding,
146 Old-Fashioned Baked Rice Pudding, 147 Chocolate Pudding
Cake, 148

Index **149**

INTRODUCTION

C*omfort foods*...the old-fashioned food favorites that memories are
made of. Moist meat loaf, creamy mac 'n cheese, real mashed potatoes with lumps here and there, crisp chicken-fried steak with thick
cream gravy, cheesy Welsh rarebit, cream of tomato soup, French toast
with maple syrup, warm sticky buns, chocolate-glazed Boston cream pie,
lemon pie with a mile-high meringue, and warm-from-the-oven oatmeal
cookies to dunk in cold milk.

Food memories are very personal and often associated with recollec-
tions of significant holidays and family events, or perhaps moments with
special people such as grandparents. Some food memories are expres-
sions of our cultural or regional backgrounds. Food memories "comfort,"
make you feel good. The fact that chicken noodle soup can aid a cold or a

bowl of warm chocolate pudding cake can defeat depression only verifies that food memories, comfort foods, are an important contribution to our physical and emotional well-being.

Many comfort foods have reappeared in recent years with the popularity of "American" and diner menus. Comfort foods are very much a part of baby boomer nostalgia. Some comfort foods have never gone out of style. But there is a difference; something has changed. We now demand foods that are low in fat and healthy as well as comforting and flavorful. Many comfort foods, though delicious, are undeniably high in fat and calories. Another change: we no longer have the luxury of time in our busy schedules to spend hours of time in meal preparation; many made-from-scratch comfort foods are just too time-consuming to prepare.

Skinny Comfort Foods to the rescue! This collection of old-fashioned favorites boasts more than 125 delicious low-fat recipes and variations that are streamlined to get you in and out of the kitchen quickly and effortlessly. And there are many pleasant surprises: recipes for Cream of Tomato and Mushroom Soups have flavors and textures that are incredibly similar to that famous brand of canned soup we all know and remember. The Sticky Buns and Pineapple Upside-Down Cake have lots of "sticky" to lick from your fingers. Cheeseburgers Supreme are so moist that juices may run down your chin. Crispy Fries are so perfectly browned and crisp you'll never guess they bypassed the deep fryer. Chocolate Buttermilk Cake is a sinful 3 layers high. Moist Carrot Cake is slathered in rich-tasting Cream Cheese Frosting. The Cheddar Cheese Soufflé soars above the soufflé dish. Baked Cereal (a famous brand again!) Pudding is so delicious you'll be back for seconds and thirds. German Potato Salad and Wilted Spinach Salad have all the flavor, almost none of the fat. Eggs Benedict and Quiche Lorraine are back on the menu! Just Plain Meat Loaf is just plain good, with leftovers planned for thick sandwiches. Some of the recipes required as many as 6 or 7 testing attempts, but we were not satisfied until results were perfect...the way we remember comfort foods yet nutritionally contemporary.

In accordance with guidelines established by the American Heart Association, none of the recipes exceeds 30 percent calories from fat, and they adhere to the nutritional criteria in the table on page xiii.

Specific nutritional information is provided for each main recipe (not variations) in this book, but please remember that nutritional data are not infallible. The nutritional analyses are derived using software highly regarded by nutritionists and dietitians, but they are meant to be used only as guidelines. Figures are based on actual laboratory values of ingredients so results may vary slightly depending upon the brand or manufacturer of an ingredient used.

Ingredients noted as "optional" or "to taste" or "as garnish" are not included in the nutritional analyses. When alternate choices or amounts of

TYPE OF RECIPE	MAXIMUM AMOUNTS PER SERVING		
	Calories	Cholesterol (mg)	Sodium (mg)
Soups, First Courses	225	50	650
One-Dish Entrees (with meat, fish, pasta rice, vegetables)	600	150	800
Main-Dish Soups Entrees, Salads Sandwiches (with meat or fish)	400	150 (175 shrimp)	800
Main-Dish Soups, Entrees, Salads (meatless)	500	125	800
Main-Dish Eggs and Cheese	400	450	800
Side-Dish Salads Pasta, Grains, Vegetables	200	50	600
Breads	200	50	600
Desserts	350	90	600

ingredients are given, the ingredient or amount listed first is used for analysis. Similarly, data is based on the first number of servings shown, where a range is given. Nutritional analyses are also based on the reduced-fat or fat-free cooking methods used in recipes; the addition of margarine, oil, or other ingredients to the recipes will invalidate data.

Other factors that can affect the accuracy of nutritional data include variability in sizes, weights, and measures of fruits, vegetables, and other foods. There is also a possible 20 percent error factor in the nutritional labeling of prepared foods.

If you have any health problems that require strict dietary requirements, it is important to consult a physician, dietitian, or nutritionist before using recipes in this or any other cookbook. Also, if you are a diabetic or require a diet that restricts calories, fat, or sodium, remember that the nutritional data may be accurate for the recipe as written but not for the food you cooked due to the variables explained above.

Variety abounds in this collection of more than 125 delicious low-fat recipes and variations. Enjoy them as you evoke your own food memories and create new ones for family and friends.

1
SOUPS

Cream of Tomato Soup

Cream of Mushroom Soup

Chicken Noodle Soup

Potato Chowder

New England Clam Chowder

Chili con Carne

Navy Bean Soup with Ham

Beef, Barley, and Vegetable Soup

Split Pea Soup with Ham

CREAM OF TOMATO SOUP

This tastes just like the favorite-brand canned tomato soup we all remember! Canned tomatoes are necessary for the flavor, so don't substitute fresh.

4 Servings (about 1¹/₄ cups each)

2 cans (14¹/₂ ounces each) no-salt whole
   tomatoes, undrained
2–3 teaspoons beef bouillon crystals
2 cups skim milk
3 tablespoons cornstarch
¹/₈ teaspoon baking soda
2 teaspoons sugar
1–2 tablespoons margarine
   Salt and pepper, to taste

1. Process tomatoes and liquid in food processor or blender until smooth; heat tomatoes and bouillon crystals in large saucepan to boiling. Mix milk and cornstarch; whisk into boiling mixture. Boil, whisking constantly, until thickened, about 1 minute.

2. Add baking soda, sugar, and margarine to soup, stirring until margarine is melted. Season to taste with salt and pepper. Ladle into bowls.

Nutritional Data

PER SERVING		EXCHANGES	
Calories:	143	Milk:	0.5
% Calories from fat:	23	Vegetable:	2.0
Fat (gm):	3.9	Fruit:	0.0
Sat. fat (gm):	0.8	Bread:	0.5
Cholesterol (mg):	2	Meat:	0.0
Sodium (mg):	628	Fat:	0.5
Protein (gm):	6.5		
Carbohydrate (gm):	22.9		

CREAM OF MUSHROOM SOUP

Creamy and rich, this soup also resembles the
favorite-brand canned soup we remember. For a richer
soup, use fat-free half-and-half instead of skim milk.

4 Servings (about 1¹/₄ cups each)

1 pound mushrooms
2 tablespoons margarine
1 cup chopped onion
2¹/₂ cups reduced-sodium chicken broth
2¹/₂ cups skim milk, divided
2 tablespoons plus 2 teaspoons cornstarch
Salt and pepper, to taste
Minced parsley leaves, as garnish

1. Slice enough mushroom caps to make 2 cups; finely chop stems and remaining mushrooms. Saute sliced mushrooms in 1 tablespoon margarine in large saucepan until browned, about 5 minutes; remove and reserve. Saute onion and chopped mushrooms in remaining 1 tablespoon margarine until onion is tender, about 5 minutes.

2. Add broth and 2 cups milk to saucepan; heat to boiling. Mix remaining ¹/₂ cup milk and cornstarch; whisk into boiling mixture. Boil, whisking constantly, until thickened, about 1 minute. Stir in reserved sliced mushrooms. Season to taste with salt and pepper. Serve in bowls; sprinkle with parsley.

Nutritional Data

PER SERVING		EXCHANGES	
Calories:	183	Milk:	0.5
% Calories from fat:	31	Vegetable:	3.0
Fat (gm):	6.5	Fruit:	0.0
Sat. fat (gm):	1.4	Bread:	0.0
Cholesterol (mg):	2.5	Meat:	0.0
Sodium (mg):	361	Fat:	1.5
Protein (gm):	11		
Carbohydrate (gm):	21.8		

CHICKEN NOODLE SOUP

A hearty, entrée soup that's quick and easy to make, using reduced-sodium canned chicken broth. If using homemade chicken broth, refrigerate it until chilled, then skim and discard fat before proceeding with the soup.

4 Servings (about 1¹/₄ cups each)

Vegetable cooking spray
4 ounces boneless, skinless chicken breast, visible fat trimmed, cut into ³/₄-inch pieces
4 ounces boneless, skinless chicken thighs, visible fat trimmed, cut into ³/₄-inch pieces
2 cups sliced celery, including some leaves
1 cup sliced carrot
1 cup sliced onion
2 cans (14¹/₂ ounces each) reduced-sodium chicken broth
1 teaspoon dried marjoram
1 bay leaf
1 cup uncooked no-yolk broad noodles
1 tablespoon minced parsley leaves
Salt and pepper, to taste

1. Spray large saucepan with cooking spray; heat over medium heat until hot. Saute chicken until browned, about 5 minutes. Add celery, carrot, and onion and saute until tender, 5 to 7 minutes.

2. Add chicken broth and herbs to saucepan; heat to boiling. Reduce heat and simmer, covered, until chicken and vegetables are tender, 15 to 20 minutes.

3. Heat soup to boiling; add noodles. Cook, uncovered, until noodles are tender, 7 to 10 minutes. Discard bay leaf. Stir in parsley; season to taste with salt and pepper.

Nutritional Data

PER SERVING		EXCHANGES	
Calories:	307	Milk:	0.0
% Calories from fat:	14	Vegetable:	1.0
Fat (gm):	5	Fruit:	0.0
Sat. fat (gm):	0.8	Bread:	2.5
Cholesterol (mg):	32.9	Meat:	2.0
Sodium (mg):	409	Fat:	0.0
Protein (gm):	22.8		
Carbohydrate (gm):	44.3		

POTATO CHOWDER

◆

A basic soup that is versatile—substitute any desired vegetables, such as carrots, zucchini, green beans, or corn, for part of the potatoes for a delectable vegetable chowder.

6 Servings (about 1 cup each)

1 cup chopped onion
1/4 cup thinly sliced celery
2 tablespoons margarine
3 tablespoons flour
2 cups reduced-sodium chicken broth
3 1/2 cups peeled, cubed Idaho potatoes
1/4–1/2 teaspoon celery seed
2 cups skim milk
Salt and pepper, to taste

1. Saute onion and celery in margarine in large saucepan until tender, 5 to 8 minutes. Stir in flour; cook over medium-low heat, stirring constantly, 1 minute.

2. Add broth, potatoes, and celery seed to saucepan; heat to boiling. Reduce heat and simmer, covered, until potatoes are tender, 10 to 15 minutes. Stir in milk; cook over medium heat until hot, 2 to 3 minutes. Season to taste with salt and pepper.

Variation

Vichyssoise: Make recipe as above, substituting chopped leek for half the onion and deleting celery and celery seed. Cool; process soup in food processor or blender until smooth. Refrigerate until chilled. Serve in bowls; sprinkle with minced fresh chives.

Nutritional Data

PER SERVING		EXCHANGES	
Calories:	212	Milk:	0.0
% Calories from fat:	17	Vegetable:	1.0
Fat (gm):	4.2	Fruit:	0.0
Sat. fat (gm):	0.9	Bread:	2.0
Cholesterol (mg):	1.3	Meat:	0.0
Sodium (mg):	210	Fat:	1.0
Protein (gm):	7.5		
Carbohydrate (gm):	37.1		

NEW ENGLAND CLAM CHOWDER

Fresh clams can be used in this fragrant clam chowder entrée; see Note following the recipe.

6 Servings

2 slices bacon
1 cup chopped onion
1 cup chopped celery
1/4 cup all-purpose flour
2 cups clam juice
2 cans (6 1/2 ounces each) diced clams, undrained
1 can (6 1/2 ounces) whole clams, undrained
1 3/4 cups peeled, cubed russet potatoes
1 teaspoon dried thyme
1 bay leaf
1 1/2–2 cups fat-free half-and-half, *or* skim milk
Salt and pepper, to taste

1. Fry bacon in large saucepan until crisp; drain well, crumble, and reserve. Drain all fat from pan; add onion and celery and saute until tender, 5 to 8 minutes. Stir in flour; cook over medium-low heat, stirring constantly, 1 minute.

2. Stir in clam juice, clams and liquid, potatoes, and herbs; heat to boiling. Reduce heat and simmer, covered, until potatoes are tender, about 15 minutes. Stir in half-and-half; cook over medium heat until hot through, about 5 minutes. Discard bay leaf; season to taste with salt and pepper.

Note

If using fresh clams, soak 3 dozen clams in cold water to cover for 30 minutes. Heat clams to boiling in a covered skillet with 1/2 cup water; boil until clams have opened, 2 to 4 minutes. Remove clams from shells; discard any clams that did not open. Strain any remaining broth through a double layer of cheesecloth and add to chowder.

Nutritional Data

PER SERVING		EXCHANGES	
Calories:	195	Milk:	0.0
% Calories from fat:	11	Vegetable:	0.0
Fat (gm):	2.3	Fruit:	0.0
Sat. fat (gm):	0.6	Bread:	1.5
Cholesterol (mg):	59.2	Meat:	1.0
Sodium (mg):	261	Fat:	0.0
Protein (gm):	13.4		
Carbohydrate (gm):	30.3		

CHILI CON CARNE

For a Southwest version of this chili, substitute black or pinto beans for the kidney beans and add 1 minced jalapeño chili. Garnish each serving with a sprinkling of finely chopped cilantro leaves.

8 Servings (about 1 cup each)

Vegetable cooking spray
1 pound 95% lean ground beef
1½ cups chopped onion
1 cup chopped green bell pepper
2 cloves garlic, minced
1–2 tablespoons chili powder
2 teaspoons dried cumin
1 teaspoon dried oregano
¼ teaspoon ground cloves
2 cans (14½ ounces each) no-salt whole tomatoes, undrained, coarsely chopped
1 can (6 ounces) reduced-sodium tomato paste
¾ cup beer, *or* reduced-sodium beef broth
1 tablespoon packed light brown sugar
2–3 teaspoons unsweetened cocoa
1 can (15 ounces) red kidney beans, rinsed, drained
Salt and pepper, to taste
½ cup shredded fat-free, *or* reduced-fat, Cheddar cheese
½ cup thinly sliced green onion and tops
½ cup fat-free, *or* reduced-fat, sour cream

1. Spray large saucepan with cooking spray; heat over medium heat until hot. Add ground beef, onion, bell pepper, and garlic; cook over medium heat until meat is brown and vegetables are tender, 5 to 8 minutes. Add chili powder, cumin, oregano, and cloves; cook 1 to 2 minutes longer.

2. Add tomatoes, tomato paste, beer, brown sugar, and cocoa to beef mixture. Heat to boiling; reduce heat and simmer, covered, 1 hour. Stir in beans and simmer, uncovered, to thicken, if desired. Season to taste with salt and pepper.

3. Spoon chili into bowls; sprinkle each with 1 tablespoon cheese, green onion, and sour cream.

Variation:

Chili Mac: In step 2, add 1 cup uncooked elbow macaroni or chili mac pasta and ½ cup water to chili after 45 minutes cooking time; heat to boiling. Reduce heat and simmer, covered, until macaroni is tender, about 15 minutes; stir in beans and simmer 5 minutes.

Nutritional Data

PER SERVING		EXCHANGES	
Calories:	220	Milk:	0.0
% Calories from fat:	13	Vegetable:	2.0
Fat (gm):	3.6	Fruit:	0.0
Sat. fat (gm):	1	Bread:	1.0
Cholesterol (mg):	32.5	Meat:	2.0
Sodium (mg):	224	Fat:	0.0
Protein (gm):	21.9		
Carbohydrate (gm):	28.7		

NAVY BEAN SOUP WITH HAM

◆

A quick-soak method is used for the beans. If you prefer soaking the beans overnight, delete step 1 and proceed with step 2 in the recipe.

6 Servings (about 1¹/₄ cups each)

8 ounces dried navy, *or* Great Northern beans, washed and sorted
Water
1¹/₂ cups cubed lean smoked ham (8 ounces), visible fat trimmed
²/₃ cup chopped onion
²/₃ cup chopped carrot
1 rib celery, thinly sliced
2 cloves garlic, minced
1 tablespoon vegetable oil
1 tablespoon flour
4 cups reduced-sodium chicken broth
1 cup water
¹/₄ teaspoon dried thyme
1 bay leaf
Salt and pepper, to taste

1. Cover beans with 2 inches of water in large saucepan; heat to boiling and boil, uncovered, 2 minutes. Remove from heat and let stand, covered, 1 hour; drain.

2. Saute ham, onion, carrot, celery, and garlic in oil in large saucepan until vegetables are tender, 5 to 8 minutes. Stir in flour; cook over medium heat 1 minute.

3. Add beans, broth, water, and herbs to the saucepan; heat to boiling. Reduce heat and simmer, covered, until beans are tender, 1¹/₄ to 1¹/₂ hours. Discard bay leaf; season to taste with salt and pepper.

Nutritional Data

PER SERVING		EXCHANGES	
Calories:	223	Milk:	0.0
% Calories from fat:	16	Vegetable:	0.0
Fat (gm):	4.0	Fruit:	0.0
Sat. fat (gm):	0.9	Bread:	2.0
Cholesterol (mg):	21.6	Meat:	2.0
Sodium (mg):	639	Fat:	0.0
Protein (gm):	20.1		
Carbohydrate (gm):	29.5		

BEEF, BARLEY, AND VEGETABLE SOUP

♦

A hearty, rib-sticking soup that is even better if made a day or so in advance. Leftover soup will thicken, so thin with beef broth or water.

8 Servings (about 1 cup each)

Vegetable cooking spray
1 pound lean beef stew meat, visible fat trimmed
1 cup chopped onion
⅔ cup sliced celery
⅔ cup chopped carrot
1 clove garlic, minced
1 tablespoon flour
4 cups water
1 can (14½ ounces) reduced-sodium beef broth
½ teaspoon dried marjoram
½ teaspoon dried thyme
1 bay leaf
1 can (14½ ounces) diced tomatoes, undrained
1 cup cut green beans (1-inch pieces)
1 cup cubed parsnips, *or* potatoes
½ cup frozen peas
½ cup quick-cooking barley
Salt and pepper, to taste

1. Spray large Dutch oven with cooking spray; heat over medium heat until hot. Cook beef over medium heat until browned, 8 to 10 minutes. Add onion, celery, carrot, and garlic; cook 5 minutes. Stir in flour; cook 1 minute.

2. Add water, beef broth, and herbs to Dutch oven; heat to boiling. Reduce heat and simmer, covered, until beef is very tender, 1 to 1½ hours.

3. Add tomatoes and liquid, green beans, and parsnips; simmer, covered, until vegetables are tender, about 10 minutes. Add peas and barley and heat to boiling; reduce heat and simmer, covered, until barley is tender, about 10 minutes. Discard bay leaf; season to taste with salt and pepper.

Nutritional Data

PER SERVING		EXCHANGES	
Calories:	187	Milk:	0.0
% Calories from fat:	16	Vegetable:	2.0
Fat (gm):	3.3	Fruit:	0.0
Sat. fat (gm):	1.1	Bread:	0.5
Cholesterol (mg):	35.4	Meat:	2.0
Sodium (mg):	153	Fat:	0.0
Protein (gm):	18.8		
Carbohydrate (gm):	21.1		

SPLIT PEA SOUP WITH HAM

A perfect main-dish soup for hearty appetites on a crisp autumn or winter day. Serve with thick slices of Garlic Bread (see p. 106).

8 Servings (about 1 cup each)

1½ cups chopped onion
1 cup chopped carrot
½ cup sliced celery
1½ cups cubed lean smoked ham (8 ounces),
    visible fat trimmed
1 tablespoon vegetable oil
6 cups water
1 can (14½ ounces) reduced-sodium
    chicken broth
1 pound dried split peas, washed and sorted
1–2 teaspoons beef bouillon crystals
1 teaspoon dried marjoram
    Salt and pepper, to taste

1. Saute onion, carrot, celery, and ham in oil in large saucepan until tender, 8 to 10 minutes. Add water, chicken broth, split peas, bouillon crystals, and marjoram; heat to boiling. Reduce heat and simmer, covered, until peas are tender, 1 to 1¼ hours. Season to taste with salt and pepper.

Nutritional Data

PER SERVING		EXCHANGES	
Calories:	264	Milk:	0.0
% Calories from fat:	11	Vegetable:	1.0
Fat (gm):	3.4	Fruit:	0.0
Sat. fat (gm):	0.6	Bread:	2.0
Cholesterol (mg):	16.2	Meat:	2.0
Sodium (mg):	513	Fat:	0.0
Protein (gm):	21.6		
Carbohydrate (gm):	39.9		

2
MEATS

Steak au Poivre

Pepper Steak

Chicken-Fried Steak

Old-Fashioned Pot Roast

Beef Bourguignonne

Beef Stroganoff

Country Beef Stew

Just Plain Meat Loaf

Salisbury Steak with Mushroom Gravy

Swedish Meatballs with Noodles

Roast Beef Hash

Mock Chicken Legs

Chop Suey

Shepherd's Pie

STEAK AU POIVRE

◆

This elegant special-occasion entrée is made with low-fat beef eye
of round steak rather than the traditional higher-fat tenderloin.
Beef eye of round steak has less than 30% calories from fat.

4 Servings

2 teaspoons crushed black peppercorns
4 beef eye of round steaks (4 ounces each),
  visible fat trimmed
  Salt, to taste
  Vegetable cooking spray
1/3 cup brandy
1/4 cup fat-free sour cream

1. Press peppercorns into steak, using about 1/4 teaspoon per side; sprinkle lightly with salt. Spray medium skillet with cooking spray; heat over medium to medium-high heat until hot. Add steaks to skillet and cook over medium heat to desired degree of doneness, 3 to 4 minutes on each side for medium. Remove steaks to serving plates.

2. Add brandy to skillet; heat to boiling. Boil, scraping bottom of skillet to loosen cooked particles. Boil until reduced to about 2 tablespoons, 2 to 3 minutes. Stir in sour cream and cook over low heat 1 to 2 minutes. Spoon sauce over steaks.

Note

A mixture of white, pink, green, and black peppercorns can be used.

Nutritional Data

PER SERVING		EXCHANGES	
Calories:	212	Milk:	0.0
% Calories from fat:	20	Vegetable:	0.0
Fat (gm):	4.5	Fruit:	0.0
Sat. fat (gm):	1.6	Bread:	0.0
Cholesterol (mg):	64	Meat:	3.5
Sodium (mg):	68	Fat:	0.0
Protein (gm):	27.7		
Carbohydrate (gm):	2.1		

PEPPER STEAK

◆

*Perfect for family meals or for casual buffet-style
entertaining. For a colorful variation, use a
combination of green, red, and yellow peppers.*

6 Servings (about 1 cup each)

Vegetable cooking spray
3 cups sliced green bell peppers
2½ cups sliced onion
4 cloves garlic, minced
1 pound beef eye of round steak, *or* sirloin
   steak, visible fat trimmed, cut into
   3 x ¼-inch strips
2 tablespoons flour
1¾ cups reduced-sodium beef broth, divided
½ cup water
1 tablespoon tomato paste
½ teaspoon Italian seasoning
2 tablespoons cornstarch
1½ cups quartered cherry tomatoes
1–2 tablespoons Worcestershire sauce
   Salt and pepper, to taste
4½ cups cooked no-yolk noodles, warm

1. Spray large skillet with cooking spray; heat over medium heat until hot. Saute bell peppers until tender, about 5 minutes; remove from pan and reserve. Add onion and garlic to skillet; saute until tender, 5 to 8 minutes.

2. Coat beef with flour and add to skillet; cook over medium to medium-low heat 3 to 5 minutes, stirring frequently. Add 1½ cups broth, water, tomato paste, and Italian seasoning; heat to boiling. Reduce heat and simmer, covered, until beef is tender, about 45 minutes, adding reserved peppers during last 10 minutes.

3. Heat pepper steak mixture to boiling. Mix cornstarch and remaining ¼ cup beef broth; stir into boiling mixture. Boil, stirring constantly, until thickened, about 1 minute. Stir in tomatoes and simmer 10 minutes. Season to taste with Worcestershire sauce, salt, and pepper. Serve with noodles.

Variation

Sweet-Sour Pepper Steak: Make recipe as above, stirring ¼ cup apricot preserves, ½ cup sliced water chestnuts, and 2 to 3 teaspoons cider vinegar in at the end. Substitute 1½ cups snow peas for half of the bell peppers and reduced-sodium soy sauce for the Worcestershire sauce.

Nutritional Data

PER SERVING		EXCHANGES	
Calories:	383	Milk:	0.0
% Calories from fat:	13	Vegetable:	3.0
Fat (gm):	5.8	Fruit:	0.0
Sat. fat (gm):	1.2	Bread:	2.5
Cholesterol (mg):	42.6	Meat:	2.5
Sodium (mg):	127	Fat:	0.0
Protein (gm):	28.7		
Carbohydrate (gm):	56.2		

CHICKEN-FRIED STEAK

◆

The beef steaks are pounded until thin for faster cooking and tenderness. Use seasoned or unseasoned breadcrumbs, as you prefer.

4 Servings

4 beef eye of round steaks (4 ounces each)
2 tablespoons flour
2 egg whites, *or* ¼ cup real egg product
¼ cup skim milk
⅓ cup dry seasoned breadcrumbs
   Vegetable cooking spray
   Salt and pepper, to taste
   Cream Gravy (see p. 25)

1. Pound steaks with flat side of mallet to ¼ inch thickness. Coat steaks lightly with flour; dip in combined egg and skim milk and coat with breadcrumbs. Spray both sides of steaks with cooking spray.

2. Spray large skillet generously with cooking spray; heat over medium heat until hot. Cook steaks over medium heat until browned, about 5 minutes on each side. Cover and cook over very low heat until steaks are tender, turning occasionally, 30 to 40 minutes. Season to taste with salt and pepper. Serve with Cream Gravy.

Nutritional Data

PER SERVING		EXCHANGES	
Calories:	349	Milk:	0.5
% Calories from fat:	29	Vegetable:	0.0
Fat (gm):	11	Fruit:	0.0
Sat. fat (gm):	3	Bread:	1.5
Cholesterol (mg):	66.2	Meat:	3.5
Sodium (mg):	309	Fat:	0.0
Protein (gm):	36.5		
Carbohydrate (gm):	23.8		

OLD-FASHIONED POT ROAST

◆

Cabbage, turnips, and sweet potatoes are other vegetable choices that can be used in this recipe—use the favorites you remember!

6 Servings

Vegetable cooking spray
2³⁄₄ pounds chuck arm pot roast, visible fat trimmed
Salt and pepper, to taste
3 medium onions, cut into wedges, divided
6 cloves garlic, minced
1¹⁄₂ cups reduced-sodium beef broth, divided
¹⁄₂ teaspoon dried thyme
1 bay leaf
1 pound Idaho, *or* red, potatoes, unpeeled, cut into 1¹⁄₂-inch pieces
8 ounces carrot cut into 1¹⁄₂-inch pieces
8 ounces rutabaga, *or* parsnip, cut into 1¹⁄₂-inch pieces
¹⁄₄ cup all-purpose flour
Salt and pepper, to taste

1. Spray large Dutch oven with cooking spray; heat over medium heat until hot. Add meat and cook over medium heat until browned, 2 to 3 minutes on each side. Remove from pan and sprinkle lightly with salt and pepper. Add half the onion and all the garlic to the pan; saute 2 to 3 minutes.

2. Return meat to pan. Add 1 cup beef broth and herbs to pan and heat to boiling. Transfer to oven and bake, covered, at 325° until meat is fork-tender, 2³⁄₄ to 3 hours. Add reserved onion and remaining vegeta-

bles to pan during last hour of cooking time, sprinkling lightly with salt and pepper. Arrange meat and vegetables on serving platter; discard bay leaf.

3. Pour meat juices into glass measure; spoon off and discard fat. Add water to juices, if necessary, to make 2 cups; heat to boiling in Dutch oven. Mix flour and remaining ½ cup beef broth; stir into boiling juices. Boil, whisking constantly, until thickened, about 1 minute; season to taste with salt and pepper. Serve gravy with pot roast and vegetables.

Note

If desired, red wine, beer, or tomato juice can be substituted for ½ cup of the beef broth.

Nutritional Data

PER SERVING		EXCHANGES	
Calories:	377	Milk:	0.0
% Calories from fat:	15	Vegetable:	2.0
Fat (gm):	6.4	Fruit:	0.0
Sat. fat (gm):	2.2	Bread:	1.5
Cholesterol (mg):	95.6	Meat:	4.0
Sodium (mg):	110	Fat:	0.0
Protein (gm):	37		
Carbohydrate (gm):	42.6		

BEEF BOURGUIGNONNE

---◆---

*I remember this French-style stew being served for company,
when ordinary beef stew was not quite fancy enough!*

6 Servings

1½ pounds beef eye of round steak, visible fat
trimmed, cut into scant 1½-inch cubes
¼ cup all-purpose flour
1 tablespoon olive, *or* vegetable, oil
1 cup Burgundy wine, *or* reduced-sodium beef
broth
1 cup water
1½ cups peeled pearl onion
3 cups cubed, *or* julienned, carrot
8 ounces medium mushrooms
1 teaspoon dried marjoram
1 teaspoon dried thyme
2 bay leaves
½ teaspoon salt
¼ teaspoon pepper
16 ounces egg noodles, cooked, warm

1. Coat beef cubes with flour; saute in oil in Dutch oven until browned on all sides, about 10 minutes. Add wine and water; heat to boiling.

2. Transfer Dutch oven to oven and bake, covered, at 350° until beef is very tender, about 2 hours. Add vegetables, herbs, and salt and pepper during last 30 minutes of baking time. Discard bay leaves. Serve over noodles.

Nutritional Data

PER SERVING		EXCHANGES	
Calories:	507	Milk:	0.0
% Calories from fat:	16	Vegetable:	2.0
Fat (gm):	8.8	Fruit:	0.0
Sat. fat (gm):	2.1	Bread:	4.0
Cholesterol (mg):	120.2	Meat:	3.0
Sodium (mg):	288	Fat:	0.0
Protein (gm):	34.9		
Carbohydrate (gm):	65		

BEEF STROGANOFF

◆

A long-ago favorite for buffet entertaining,
this dish still enjoys deserved popularity.

4 Servings

1 pound beef eye of round, *or* sirloin steak,
   visible fat trimmed, cut into 1½ x ½-inch
   strips
1 tablespoon margarine
3 cups sliced mushrooms
½ cup sliced onion
2 cloves garlic, minced
2 tablespoons flour
1½ cups reduced-sodium beef broth
1 teaspoon Dijon-style mustard
¼ teaspoon dried thyme
½ cup fat-free sour cream
   Salt and pepper, to taste
3 cups cooked no-yolk noodles, warm
   Finely chopped parsley leaves, as garnish

1. Saute beef in margarine in large saucepan until browned on all sides, about 5 minutes; remove from pan. Add mushrooms, onion, and garlic; saute until tender, 5 to 8 minutes. Stir in flour and cook, stirring, 1 to 2 minutes.

2. Add reserved beef, beef broth, mustard, and thyme leaves. Heat to boiling; reduce heat and simmer, covered, until beef is tender, 20 to 25 minutes. Reduce heat to low; stir in sour cream and cook 2 to 3 minutes. Season to taste with salt and pepper. Serve over noodles; sprinkle with parsley.

Nutritional Data

PER SERVING		EXCHANGES	
Calories:	423	Milk:	0.0
% Calories from fat:	21	Vegetable:	1.0
Fat (gm):	10	Fruit:	0.0
Sat. fat (gm):	2.2	Bread:	2.5
Cholesterol (mg):	64	Meat:	4.0
Sodium (mg):	167	Fat:	0.0
Protein (gm):	39		
Carbohydrate (gm):	45.1		

COUNTRY BEEF STEW

◆

Simmer it for a long time for old-fashioned goodness.
Use your family's favorite vegetables, and serve the
thick stew over cooked noodles in shallow bowls.

4 Servings (about 1 cup each)

Vegetable cooking spray
1 pound lean beef stew meat, visible fat trimmed
1/2 cup chopped onion
1/2 cup chopped celery
2 cloves garlic, minced
1 cup reduced-sodium beef broth
1/2 cup dry red wine, *or* reduced-sodium beef broth
1 tablespoon tomato paste
1/2 teaspoon dried thyme
1/2 teaspoon dried rosemary
1 bay leaf
1 cup unpeeled, cubed potatoes
1 cup sliced carrot (1-inch pieces)
1/2 cup cubed parsnip, *or* turnip
1/2 cup frozen peas
2 tablespoons flour
1/4 cup cold water
Salt and pepper, to taste

1. Spray large saucepan with cooking spray; heat over medium heat until hot. Add beef and cook until browned, 5 to 8 minutes. Add onion, celery, and garlic; cook until tender, about 5 minutes.

2. Add beef broth, wine, tomato paste, and herbs to saucepan; heat to boiling. Reduce heat and simmer, covered, until beef is tender, 1 1/2 to 2 hours. Add remaining vegetables; simmer, covered, 30 minutes.

3. Heat stew to boiling. Mix flour and water and stir into stew; boil, stirring constantly, until thickened. Discard bay leaf; season to taste with salt and pepper.

Nutritional Data

PER SERVING		EXCHANGES	
Calories:	326	Milk:	0.0
% Calories from fat:	16	Vegetable:	2.0
Fat (gm):	5.8	Fruit:	0.0
Sat. fat (gm):	2	Bread:	1.5
Cholesterol (mg):	70.9	Meat:	3.0
Sodium (mg):	171	Fat:	0.0
Protein (gm):	33.5		
Carbohydrate (gm):	29.6		

JUST PLAIN MEAT LOAF

Moist, the way you remember, with plenty of leftovers for sandwiches, too! Add sauteed mushrooms and a teaspoon or two of horseradish, if you like, and serve with Real Mashed Potatoes (see p. 78).

6 Servings (2 generous slices each)

   1 cup quick-cooking oats
  1/2 cup skim milk
   2 egg whites, *or* 1/4 cup real egg product
  1/4 cup catsup, *or* chili sauce
  1/2 cup chopped onion
  1/4 cup chopped green bell pepper
   1 clove garlic, minced
   1 teaspoon dried Italian herbs
1 1/2 pounds ground beef eye of round steak, *or* 95% lean ground beef
  3/4 teaspoon salt
  1/2 teaspoon pepper

1. Mix oats, milk, egg whites, catsup, onion, bell pepper, garlic, and herbs in medium bowl. Mix in beef, salt, and pepper until blended.

2. Pat mixture into ungreased loaf pan, 9 x 5 inches, or shape into a loaf in baking pan. Bake at 350° until juices run clear and meat thermometer registers 170°, about 1 hour. Let stand in pan 5 minutes; remove to serving plate.

Note

For decadent comfort, sprinkle meat loaf with 1/2 cup (2 ounces) shredded fat-free Cheddar cheese or 1/4 cup catsup during last 10 minutes of baking time.

Variation

Stuffed Green Peppers: Cut 6 medium green bell peppers lengthwise into halves; discard seeds. Immerse peppers in boiling water and cook 3 minutes; drain well on paper toweling. Make meat mixture as above, substituting 1 cup cooked rice for the oats and tomato sauce for the catsup.

Fill peppers with beef mixture and place in baking pan. Bake, covered, at 350° until beef mixture is no longer pink in the center, about 45 minutes. Serve with tomato sauce, if desired.

Nutritional Data

PER SERVING		EXCHANGES	
Calories:	241	Milk:	0.0
% Calories from fat:	21	Vegetable:	0.0
Fat (gm):	5.5	Fruit:	0.0
Sat. fat (gm):	1.8	Bread:	1.0
Cholesterol (mg):	64.3	Meat:	3.0
Sodium (mg):	489	Fat:	0.0
Protein (gm):	31.2		
Carbohydrate (gm):	15.3		

SALISBURY STEAK WITH MUSHROOM GRAVY

The rich Mushroom Gravy is a flavorful complement to perfectly cooked, moist salisbury steaks.

4 Servings

1 pound ground beef eye of round steak, *or* 95% lean ground beef
2–4 tablespoons finely chopped onion
3 tablespoons water
1/2 teaspoon salt
1/4 teaspoon pepper
Vegetable cooking spray
Mushroom Gravy (recipe follows)

1. Mix ground beef, onion, water, salt, and pepper in medium bowl just until blended. Shape mixture into four 1-inch-thick oval patties.

2. Spray large skillet with cooking spray; heat over medium heat until hot. Cook Salisbury Steaks to desired degree of doneness, 3 to 4 minutes per side for medium. Serve with Mushroom Gravy.

Mushroom Gravy

Makes about 1¹/₄ cups

Vegetable cooking spray
1 cup sliced mushrooms
¹/₄ cup finely chopped onion
2 tablespoons flour
1 cup reduced-sodium beef broth
Salt and pepper, to taste

1. Spray medium saucepan with cooking spray; heat over medium heat until hot. Add mushrooms and onion to saucepan; cook, covered, over medium-low heat until mushrooms are wilted, about 5 minutes. Cook, uncovered, over medium heat until onions are tender, 3 to 4 minutes. Stir in flour; cook 1 to 2 minutes longer.

2. Add beef broth and heat to boiling; boil, stirring constantly, until thickened. Season to taste with salt and pepper.

Nutritional Data

PER SERVING		EXCHANGES	
Calories:	184	Milk:	0.0
% Calories from fat:	24	Vegetable:	1.0
Fat (gm):	4.6	Fruit:	0.0
Sat. fat (gm):	1.7	Bread:	0.0
Cholesterol (mg):	64	Meat:	3.0
Sodium (mg):	341	Fat:	0.0
Protein (gm):	28.7		
Carbohydrate (gm):	5.2		

SWEDISH MEATBALLS WITH NOODLES

---◆---

Serve as a one-dish meal, or just shape the meat mixture into 48 meatballs for appetizer servings for 12 to 16 people.

4 Servings

  1 pound 95% lean ground beef
  1/2 cup finely chopped onion
  1/2 cup unseasoned dry breadcrumbs
  1/3 cup skim milk
  2 egg whites, *or* 1/4 cup real egg product
  1 tablespoon minced parsley leaves
  1/2–1 teaspoon dried dill weed
  1/4 teaspoon ground allspice
  Pinch ground cardamom
  1/2 teaspoon salt
  1/8 teaspoon pepper
  Cream Gravy (recipe follows)
  Finely chopped fresh dill weed, *or* parsley, as garnish
  3 cups cooked no-yolk noodles, warm

1. Combine ground beef, onion, breadcrumbs, milk, egg whites, parsley, dried dill weed, allspice, cardamom, salt, and pepper; shape mixture into 24 meatballs. Bake meatballs in baking pan at 425° until browned and no longer pink in the center, 15 to 20 minutes.

2. Arrange meatballs in serving bowl; pour Cream Gravy over and sprinkle with dill weed. Serve over noodles.

Cream Gravy

Makes about 2 cups

  2 tablespoons margarine
  1/4 cup all-purpose flour
  2 cups skim milk, *or* fat-free half-and-half
  1/2 teaspoon beef bouillon crystals
  1/4 cup fat-free sour cream
  Salt and pepper, to taste

1. Melt margarine in medium saucepan; stir in flour and cook over medium-low heat 1 minute, stirring constantly. Whisk in milk, bouillon crystals, and drippings from baking pan; heat to boiling. Boil, stirring constantly, until thickened, about 1 minute. Stir in sour cream and cook 1 to 2 minutes; season to taste with salt and pepper.

Nutritional Data

PER SERVING		EXCHANGES	
Calories:	497	Milk:	0.5
% Calories from fat:	24	Vegetable:	0.0
Fat (gm):	13	Fruit:	0.0
Sat. fat (gm):	3.6	Bread:	3.5
Cholesterol (mg):	67.3	Meat:	3.5
Sodium (mg):	814	Fat:	0.0
Protein (gm):	37.9		
Carbohydrate (gm):	56.6		

ROAST BEEF HASH

Any leftover beef or pork can be used in this recipe as long as it is a lean cut and trimmed of visible fat; shred or cut into cubes.

4 Servings (about 1 cup each)

Vegetable cooking spray
½ cup chopped onion
½ cup chopped green bell pepper
2 cloves garlic, minced
2 cups (8 ounces) shredded or cubed cooked lean beef
2 cups peeled and cubed cooked potatoes
½ teaspoon dried marjoram
¼ teaspoon dried thyme
Salt and pepper, to taste

1. Coat large skillet with cooking spray; heat over medium heat until hot. Saute onion, bell pepper, and garlic until tender.

2. Add beef and potatoes to skillet; sprinkle with herbs. Cook over medium heat until meat and potatoes are browned, about 10 minutes, stirring occasionally. Season to taste with salt and pepper.

Variations

Corned Beef Hash: Substitute corned beef for roast beef. Use only lean parts of the corned beef and trim visible fat.

Mexican Hash: Make recipe as above, substituting a sliced poblano chili for the bell pepper and oregano for the marjoram. Sprinkle hash with finely chopped cilantro leaves; serve with salsa and warm tortillas.

Nutritional Data

PER SERVING		EXCHANGES	
Calories:	244	Milk:	0.0
% Calories from fat:	22	Vegetable:	1.0
Fat (gm):	6	Fruit:	0.0
Sat. fat (gm):	2.3	Bread:	1.5
Cholesterol (mg):	50.7	Meat:	2.0
Sodium (mg):	44	Fat:	0.0
Protein (gm):	19.9		
Carbohydrate (gm):	27.5		

MOCK CHICKEN LEGS

Looking a little like lumpy chicken legs, these kabobs are also known as City Chicken. Use any combination of beef, pork, or veal as long as the cuts are lean and trimmed of visible fat.

6 Servings

    1 pound pork tenderloin, trimmed of visible fat
    8 ounces beef sirloin steak, trimmed of
       visible fat
  1/4 cup all-purpose flour
       Vegetable cooking spray
       Water
       Salt and pepper, to taste
       Cream Gravy (see p. 25)
 4 1/2 cups cooked rice, *or* no-yolk noodles, warm

1. Cut meats into 1-inch cubes; assemble on small wooden skewers, alternating kinds of meat. Coat meat with flour; let stand at room temperature 15 minutes.

2. Spray medium skillet with cooking spray; heat over medium heat until hot. Cook kabobs over medium to medium-low heat until well browned on all sides, about 10 minutes.

3. Add 1/2 inch water to skillet; heat to boiling. Reduce heat and simmer, covered, until meat is fork tender, 15 to 20 minutes. Remove from skillet; season to taste with salt and pepper. Serve with Cream Gravy on rice or noodles.

Nutritional Data

PER SERVING		EXCHANGES	
Calories:	397	Milk:	0.5
% Calories from fat:	20	Vegetable:	0.0
Fat (gm):	8.7	Fruit:	0.0
Sat. fat (gm):	2.5	Bread:	2.5
Cholesterol (mg):	66.6	Meat:	3.0
Sodium (mg):	140	Fat:	0.0
Protein (gm):	30.7		
Carbohydrate (gm):	46.3		

CHOP SUEY

*Bead molasses adds the traditional color
and flavor accent to this dish.*

4 Servings

1 pound pork tenderloin, cut into 1-inch cubes
1 tablespoon vegetable oil
2 cups thinly sliced Chinese cabbage, *or* 1 cup
   sliced celery
1 cup sliced mushrooms
1 cup chopped onion
1 cup chopped red or green bell pepper
2 cloves minced garlic
$1/2$ cup oriental broth, *or* reduced-sodium
   chicken broth
2 tablespoons cornstarch
$1/2$–1 tablespoon bead molasses
2 cups fresh, *or* rinsed, canned, bean sprouts
$1/2$–1 can (8 ounces) bamboo shoots, rinsed, drained
$1/2$–1 can (8 ounces) water chestnuts, rinsed, drained
   Reduced-sodium soy sauce, to taste
   Salt and pepper, to taste
3 cups cooked rice, *or* 2 cups crisp chow mein
   noodles

1. Stir-fry pork in hot oil in wok or large skillet until browned, 3 to 5 minutes. Add cabbage, mushrooms, onion, bell pepper, and garlic; stir-fry until vegetables are crisp-tender, 3 to 5 minutes longer.

2. Mix oriental broth, cornstarch, and molasses; stir into wok and heat to boiling. Boil, stirring constantly, until thickened, 1 to 2 minutes. Stir in bean sprouts, bamboo shoots, and water chestnuts; cook until hot through, 1 to 2 minutes. Season to taste with soy sauce, salt, and pepper. Serve over warm rice or crisp chow mein noodles.

Nutritional Data

PER SERVING		EXCHANGES	
Calories:	428	Milk:	0.0
% Calories from fat:	18	Vegetable:	3.0
Fat (gm):	8.4	Fruit:	0.0
Sat. fat (gm):	2	Bread:	2.5
Cholesterol (mg):	65.4	Meat:	3.0
Sodium (mg):	467	Fat:	0.0
Protein (gm):	31.8		
Carbohydrate (gm):	56.8		

SHEPHERD'S PIE

◆

Usually the recipient of the week's leftovers, this hearty stew may be different each time it is made.

Serves 6

1½ pounds boneless lamb leg steaks, visible fat trimmed, cut into ½-inch cubes
1 tablespoon margarine
¾ cup chopped onion
¾ cup chopped green bell pepper
½ cup chopped celery
3 cloves garlic, minced
3 tablespoons flour
2½ cups reduced-sodium beef broth
1½ cups sliced carrot
1 tablespoon tomato paste
½ teaspoon dried rosemary
¼–½ teaspoon dried thyme
1 bay leaf
¾ cup frozen peas
Salt and pepper, to taste
2 cups Real Mashed Potatoes (½ recipe, see p. 78)

1. Saute lamb in margarine in large saucepan until browned on all sides, 5 to 8 minutes; remove from pan. Add onion, bell pepper, celery, and garlic; saute until tender, 8 to 10 minutes. Stir in flour; cook over medium heat 1 to 2 minutes, stirring constantly.

2. Return lamb to saucepan; add broth, carrot, tomato paste, and herbs. Heat to boiling; reduce heat and simmer, covered, until lamb is tender, about 25 minutes, adding peas during last 5 minutes cooking time. Discard bay leaf; season to taste with salt and pepper.

3. Pour stew into 1½ quart casserole. Spoon Real Mashed Potatoes around edge of casserole. Bake at 400° until potatoes are browned, about 10 minutes.

Nutritional Data

PER SERVING		EXCHANGES	
Calories:	274	Milk:	
% Calories from fat:	27	Vegetable:	2.0
Fat (gm):	8.4	Fruit:	
Sat. fat (gm):	2.3	Bread:	1.0
Cholesterol (mg):	48.5	Meat:	2.5
Sodium (mg):	179	Fat:	0.5
Protein (gm):	21.7		
Carbohydrate (gm):	28.5		

3
POULTRY

Crisp Oven-Fried Chicken

Roast Chicken with Cornbread Stuffing

Chicken Cordon Bleu

Chicken à la King in Toast Cups

Chicken Paprikash

Chicken Cacciatore

Chicken Stew with Parsley Dumplings

Chicken Fricassee

Glazed Cornish Hens with Wild Rice

Turkey Divan

Turkey Pot Pie

CRISP OVEN-FRIED CHICKEN

A blend of corn flakes and breadcrumbs gives this chicken a perfect crisp coating and golden color. Serve with Real Mashed Potatoes and Cream Gravy, if you like (see pp. 78, 25), substituting chicken bouillon crystals for the beef in the gravy.

6 Servings

4 egg whites, *or* ½ cup real egg product
¼ cup 2% milk
6 skinless chicken breast halves (about 6 ounces each)
¼ cup all-purpose flour
1½ cups finely crushed corn flakes
¾ cup dry unseasoned breadcrumbs
  Butter-flavor vegetable cooking spray
  Salt and pepper, to taste

1. Beat egg whites and milk in shallow bowl until blended. Coat chicken breasts with flour; dip in egg mixture, then coat generously with combined corn flakes and breadcrumbs.

2. Spray baking pan with cooking spray. Place chicken, meat sides up, in baking pan; spray generously with cooking spray and sprinkle lightly with salt and pepper. Bake at 350° until chicken is browned and juices run clear, 45 to 60 minutes.

Note

If desired, ½ teaspoon each dried rosemary and sage and ¼ teaspoon dried thyme can be added to the corn flake mixture.

Nutritional Data

PER SERVING		EXCHANGES	
Calories:	387	Milk:	0.0
% Calories from fat:	13	Vegetable:	0.0
Fat (gm):	5.4	Fruit:	0.0
Sat. fat (gm):	1.5	Bread:	2.5
Cholesterol (mg):	104.2	Meat:	4.0
Sodium (mg):	557	Fat:	0.0
Protein (gm):	44.8		
Carbohydrate (gm):	36		

ROAST CHICKEN WITH CORNBREAD STUFFING

Avoid eating the crisp roasted skin on the chicken if you can, as the skin contains many fat calories. We've chosen to bake the stuffing in a casserole; if baked in the chicken, it would absorb unwanted fat from the chicken juices. White or wholewheat bread stuffing mix can be substituted for the cornbread stuffing.

6 Servings (with about 2/3 cup stuffing each)

1	roasting chicken (about 3 pounds)
	Vegetable cooking spray
1½	teaspoons dried rosemary, divided
1½	cups thinly sliced celery
¾	cup chopped onion
¼	cup coarsely chopped pecans (optional)
¾	teaspoon dried sage
¼	teaspoon dried thyme
3	cups cornbread stuffing mix
1½	cups reduced-sodium chicken broth
	Salt and pepper, to taste
2	egg whites, *or* ¼ cup real egg product

1. Spray chicken with cooking spray; sprinkle with 1 teaspoon rosemary. Roast chicken on rack in roasting pan at 375° until meat thermometer inserted in thickest part of thigh, away from bone, registers 170° (chicken leg will move freely and juices will run clear), about 1½ hours. Let chicken stand 10 minutes before carving.

2. Spray medium skillet with cooking spray; heat over medium heat until hot. Saute celery, onion, and pecans until vegetables are tender, 3 to 5 minutes. Stir in sage, thyme, and remaining ½ teaspoon rosemary; cook over medium heat 1 to 2 minutes.

3. Add vegetable mixture to stuffing mix in large bowl; add chicken broth and toss. Season to taste with salt and pepper. Mix in egg whites. Spoon stuffing into sprayed 2-quart casserole. Bake, covered, in oven with chicken during last 30 to 45 minutes roasting time.

Variation

Pork Chops with Bread Stuffing: Make stuffing as above, substituting white or wholewheat stuffing mix for the cornbread mix. Trim 6 loin pork chops (about 5 ounces each) of visible fat; cook in lightly sprayed skillet until well browned, about 5 minutes on each side. Arrange pork chops on top of stuffing in casserole; bake, covered, at 350° until pork chops are tender, 30 to 40 minutes.

Nutritional Data

PER SERVING		EXCHANGES	
Calories:	258	Milk:	0.0
% Calories from fat:	22	Vegetable:	0.5
Fat (gm):	6.1	Fruit:	0.0
Sat. fat (gm):	1.6	Bread:	1.5
Cholesterol (mg):	57.9	Meat:	2.5
Sodium (mg):	548	Fat:	0.0
Protein (gm):	24.4		
Carbohydrate (gm):	25.3		

CHICKEN CORDON BLEU

This recipe was once the ultimate in gourmet dining.
The ham-and-cheese-stuffed chicken breasts are
still delicious even in their skinniest form!

6 Servings

6 boneless, skinless chicken breast halves
  (4 ounces each)
4 ounces sliced fat-free Swiss cheese
3 ounces lean smoked ham
  Flour
2 egg whites, beaten
1/3 cup dry unseasoned breadcrumbs
  Vegetable cooking spray

1. Pound chicken breasts with flat side of meat mallet until very thin and even in thickness. Layer cheese and ham on chicken breasts, cutting to fit. Roll up chicken and secure with toothpicks.

2. Coat chicken rolls lightly with flour; dip in egg and coat in breadcrumbs. Spray rolls generously with cooking spray and cook in skillet over medium heat until browned on all sides, 8 to 10 minutes.

3. Bake chicken, uncovered, at 375° in baking pan until cooked through, about 30 minutes.

Nutritional Data

PER SERVING		EXCHANGES	
Calories:	210	Milk:	0.0
% Calories from fat:	18	Vegetable:	0.0
Fat (gm):	3.9	Fruit:	0.0
Sat. fat (gm):	1.1	Bread:	0.0
Cholesterol (mg):	73.2	Meat:	4.0
Sodium (mg):	540	Fat:	0.0
Protein (gm):	34.6		
Carbohydrate (gm):	6.3		

CHICKEN À LA KING IN TOAST CUPS

Make this comforting dish with half-chicken breasts, half lean ham if you like. Serve in toast cups, over toasted slices of a hearty multigrain bread, or over fluffy baked potatoes.

4 Servings (about 1/2 cup and 2 toast cups each)

2 1/2 tablespoons margarine
1/2 cup chopped green bell pepper
1 1/2 cups sliced mushrooms
1/3 cup all-purpose flour
1 1/4 cups reduced-sodium chicken broth
1 1/4 cups skim milk, *or* fat-free half-and-half
2 tablespoons dry sherry (optional)
2 cups cubed cooked chicken breast (10 to 12 ounces)
1/2 cup frozen peas, thawed
1 jar (2 ounces) chopped pimiento, rinsed, drained
Salt and pepper, to taste
Toast Cups (recipe follows)
Minced parsley leaves, as garnish

1. Melt margarine in large saucepan; saute bell pepper 2 to 3 minutes. Add mushrooms and saute until tender, 3 to 4 minutes (do not brown). Stir in flour; cook over medium-low heat, stirring constantly, 1 minute.

2. Stir broth, milk, and sherry into saucepan; heat to boiling. Boil, stirring constantly, until thickened, about 1 minute. Stir in chicken, peas, and pimiento; cook until hot through, 3 to 4 minutes. Season to taste with salt and pepper.

3. Arrange toast cups on plates; fill each with about ½ cup chicken mixture. Sprinkle with parsley.

Toast Cups

Vegetable cooking spray
8 slices wholewheat, *or* white, bread, crusts trimmed

1. Spray 8 muffin cups and 1 side of bread slices with cooking spray. Press bread slices, sprayed sides up, in muffin cups with 4 corners sticking up.

2. Bake at 350° until browned, 10 to 15 minutes. Serve warm.

Variation

Ham à la King: Substitute 10 to 12 ounces cubed, trimmed lean smoked ham for the chicken. Serve over squares of cornbread.

Nutritional Data

PER SERVING		EXCHANGES	
Calories:	386	Milk:	0.0
% Calories from fat:	24	Vegetable:	1.0
Fat (gm):	11.7	Fruit:	0.0
Sat. fat (gm):	2.3	Bread:	2.5
Cholesterol (mg):	55.7	Meat:	3.0
Sodium (mg):	578	Fat:	0.5
Protein (gm):	32.1		
Carbohydrate (gm):	39.1		

CHICKEN PAPRIKASH

♦

Lean veal can be used in this recipe instead of chicken.

4 Servings

1 pound boneless, skinless chicken breast, cut
  into scant 1-inch cubes
1 tablespoon margarine
1 cup chopped onion
4 cloves garlic, minced
1/2 cup reduced-sodium chicken broth
1/4 cup dry white wine
1 cup chopped tomato
1 teaspoon paprika
2 tablespoons flour
1/4 cup water
1/2 cup fat-free sour cream
  Salt and white pepper, to taste
3 cups cooked no-yolk noodles, warm
  Finely chopped parsley leaves, as garnish

1. Saute chicken in margarine in large saucepan until browned. Add onion and garlic and saute until tender, about 5 minutes. Add chicken broth, wine, tomato, and paprika and heat to boiling; reduce heat and simmer, covered, until chicken is tender, 15 to 20 minutes.

2. Heat mixture to boiling. Mix flour and water; stir into boiling stew. Boil, stirring constantly, until thickened, about 1 minute. Reduce heat to low; stir in sour cream and cook 2 to 3 minutes. Season to taste with salt and white pepper. Serve over noodles; sprinkle with parsley.

Nutritional Data

PER SERVING		EXCHANGES	
Calories:	416	Milk:	0.0
% Calories from fat:	18	Vegetable:	1.0
Fat (gm):	8.4	Fruit:	0.0
Sat. fat (gm):	1.4	Bread:	3.0
Cholesterol (mg):	69	Meat:	3.0
Sodium (mg):	139	Fat:	0.0
Protein (gm):	35.9		
Carbohydrate (gm):	47.9		

CHICKEN CACCIATORE

Of Italian origin, Chicken Cacciatore is also known as Hunter's Stew. Any game brought back from the hunt was used in the dish, which varied slightly from kitchen to kitchen.

4 Servings

8 ounces boneless, skinless chicken breast
8 ounces boneless, skinless chicken thighs
2 teaspoons dried basil, divided
1/2 teaspoon dried oregano
1/4 teaspoon garlic powder
   Olive oil cooking spray
   Salt and pepper, to taste
1 cup chopped onion
1 cup chopped green bell pepper
6 cloves garlic, minced
3 cups medium mushrooms, cut into quarters
2 cans (14 1/2 ounces each) reduced-sodium whole tomatoes, undrained, coarsely chopped
1/2 cup dry red, *or* white, wine
1 bay leaf
4 teaspoons cornstarch
2 tablespoons water
   Salt and pepper, to taste
3 cups cooked no-yolk broad noodles
   Finely chopped basil, *or* parsley leaves, as garnish

1. Cut chicken into serving-size pieces; sprinkle with combined 1 teaspoon basil, oregano, and garlic powder. Spray large skillet with cooking spray; heat over medium heat until hot. Cook chicken on medium heat until browned, 5 to 8 minutes; remove from skillet and sprinkle with salt and pepper.

2. Add onion, pepper, and garlic to skillet; saute 3 to 4 minutes. Add mushrooms, tomatoes with liquid, wine, and bay leaf; heat to boiling. Add reserved chicken; reduce heat and simmer, covered, until chicken is tender, 20 to 30 minutes.

3. Heat to boiling; stir in combined cornstarch and water. Boil, stirring constantly, until thickened. Discard bay leaf; season to taste with salt and pepper. Serve chicken and sauce over noodles; sprinkle with basil.

Note

4 skinless chicken breast halves (6 ounces each) can be substituted for the boneless breasts and thighs, if desired.

Nutritional Data

PER SERVING		EXCHANGES	
Calories:	411	Milk:	0.0
% Calories from fat:	15	Vegetable:	4.0
Fat (gm):	7.2	Fruit:	0.0
Sat. fat (gm):	1.7	Bread:	2.0
Cholesterol (mg):	65.5	Meat:	3.0
Sodium (mg):	199	Fat:	0.0
Protein (gm):	30.9		
Carbohydrate (gm):	53.7		

CHICKEN STEW WITH PARSLEY DUMPLINGS

For variation, delete the dumplings and serve this savory stew over noodles or Real Mashed Potatoes (see p. 78).

6 Servings

Vegetable cooking spray
1 cup chopped onion
3 carrots, cut into 3/4-inch pieces
1/2 cup sliced celery
3 cups reduced-sodium chicken broth, divided
1 1/2 cups boneless, skinless chicken breast halves, cut into 1-inch pieces
1/2–3/4 teaspoon dried sage
1/2 cup frozen peas
2 tablespoons finely chopped parsley leaves
5 tablespoons flour
Salt and pepper, to taste
Parsley Dumplings (recipe follows)

1. Spray large saucepan with cooking spray; heat over medium heat until hot. Saute onion, carrot, and celery 5 minutes. Add 2 1/2 cups chicken broth, chicken, and sage; heat to boiling. Reduce heat and simmer, covered, until chicken is cooked and vegetables tender, 10 to 15 minutes.

2. Stir peas and parsley into stew; heat to boiling. Mix flour and remaining ½ cup chicken broth; stir into stew. Boil, stirring constantly, until thickened, 1 to 2 minutes. Season to taste with salt and pepper.

3. Spoon dumpling dough into 6 mounds on top of boiling chicken and vegetables (do not drop directly in liquid). Reduce heat and simmer, covered, 10 minutes. Simmer, uncovered, 10 minutes longer.

Parsley Dumplings

  ³/₄ cup all-purpose flour
   1 teaspoon baking powder
  ¼ teaspoon salt
  1½ tablespoons vegetable shortening
  ⅓ cup 2% milk
   1 tablespoon finely chopped parsley

1. Combine flour, baking powder, and salt in small bowl. Cut in shortening with pastry blender until mixture resembles coarse crumbs. Stir in milk to make a soft dough; stir in parsley.

Nutritional Data

PER SERVING		EXCHANGES	
Calories:	233	Milk:	0.0
% Calories from fat:	20	Vegetable:	2.0
Fat (gm):	5.1	Fruit:	0.0
Sat. fat (gm):	1.4	Bread:	1.0
Cholesterol (mg):	35.5	Meat:	1.5
Sodium (mg):	383	Fat:	0.5
Protein (gm):	19.2		
Carbohydrate (gm):	26.7		

CHICKEN FRICASSEE

Cloves and bay leaf add a flavor update to
this dish; more traditional seasonings of rosemary
and thyme can be substituted, if desired.

6 Servings

Vegetable cooking spray
6 skinless chicken breast halves (about 6 ounces each)
1 medium onion, cut into wedges
4 medium carrots, cut into 1-inch pieces
4 ribs celery, cut into 1-inch pieces
2 cloves garlic, minced
3 tablespoons flour
2 cans (14$1/2$ ounces each) reduced-sodium chicken broth
16 whole cloves
2 bay leaves
1 teaspoon lemon juice
$1/2$ teaspoon sugar
$1/2$ teaspoon salt
$1/4$ teaspoon pepper
12 ounces cooked fettuccine, *or* no-yolk noodles, warm
Minced parsley leaves, as garnish

1. Spray large skillet or Dutch oven with cooking spray; heat over medium heat until hot. Cook chicken until browned, about 8 minutes. Remove from skillet. Add vegetables to skillet; saute 5 minutes. Stir in flour and cook 1 minute, stirring constantly.

2. Return chicken to skillet. Add chicken broth, cloves and bay leaves tied in cheesecloth, lemon juice, and sugar. Heat to boiling; reduce heat and simmer, covered, until chicken is tender, about 20 minutes. Simmer, uncovered, until sauce is thickened to medium consistency, about 10 minutes. Discard spice packet; stir in salt and pepper.

3. Serve chicken and vegetables over pasta; sprinkle with parsley.

Nutritional Data

PER SERVING		EXCHANGES	
Calories:	349	Milk:	0.0
% Calories from fat:	11	Vegetable:	1.0
Fat (gm):	4.2	Fruit:	0.0
Sat. fat (gm):	0.8	Bread:	3.0
Cholesterol (mg):	48.5	Meat:	2.0
Sodium (mg):	28	Fat:	0.0
Protein (gm):	28		
Carbohydrate (gm):	48.4		

GLAZED CORNISH HENS WITH WILD RICE

Cornish hens are roasted to golden perfection, marmalade-glazed, and served with a fruited wild-and-white rice for company fare!

4 Servings

2 Rock Cornish game hens (1 to 1¼ pounds each)
Vegetable cooking spray
Paprika
⅓ cup orange marmalade
¼ cup sliced green onion and tops
¼ cup sliced celery
1 package (6.25 ounces) fast-cooking long-grain white-and-wild rice, spice packet discarded
1 can (14½ ounces) reduced-sodium chicken broth
1 can (11 ounces) mandarin orange segments, drained
2 tablespoons raisins
2 tablespoons finely chopped mint, *or* parsley, leaves
Salt and pepper, to taste
2 tablespoons toasted pecan halves (optional)

1. Cut hens into halves with poultry shears and place cut sides down on rack in roasting pan. Spray with cooking spray and sprinkle with paprika. Roast at 350° until thickest parts are fork-tender and drumstick meat feels soft when pressed, 1 to 1¼ hours. Baste frequently with marmalade during last 30 minutes of cooking time.

2. Spray medium saucepan with cooking spray; heat over medium heat until hot. Saute green onion and celery until tender, about 5 minutes. Add rice and chicken broth and heat to boiling. Reduce heat and simmer, covered, until rice is tender, about 5 minutes. Stir in orange segments, raisins, and mint; cook 2 to 3 minutes longer. Season to taste with salt and pepper.

3. Spoon rice onto serving platter and sprinkle with pecans; arrange hens on rice.

Nutritional Data

PER SERVING		EXCHANGES	
Calories:	473	Milk:	0.0
% Calories from fat:	21	Vegetable:	0.0
Fat (gm):	11.1	Fruit:	0.5
Sat. fat (gm):	0.8	Bread:	3.5
Cholesterol (mg):	40.1	Meat:	3.0
Sodium (mg):	217	Fat:	0.5
Protein (gm):	31.4		
Carbohydrate (gm):	63.5		

TURKEY DIVAN

For real convenience, assemble this casserole in advance and refrigerate up to 24 hours. Then sprinkle with breadcrumbs and bake until bubbly, about 25 minutes.

4 Servings

1½ cups cubed cooked turkey, *or* chicken breast (12 ounces)
2 cups broccoli florets, cooked until crisp-tender
⅓ cup chopped onion
1 tablespoon margarine
⅓ cup all-purpose flour
¾ cup reduced-sodium chicken broth
¾ cup fat-free, half-and-half, *or* skim milk
¼ cup dry white wine, *or* skim milk
¼–½ teaspoon dried savory
¼ teaspoon dried marjoram
2–3 pinches ground nutmeg
1 cup (4 ounces) shredded fat-free Swiss cheese
Salt, cayenne, and white pepper, to taste
3–4 tablespoons dry unseasoned breadcrumbs

1. Arrange turkey and broccoli in 10 x 6-inch baking dish.

2. Saute onion in margarine in medium saucepan until tender, 2 to 3 minutes. Mix flour and chicken broth until smooth; stir into saucepan with half-and-half and wine. Heat to boiling; boil, whisking constantly, until thickened, about 1 minute. Reduce heat to low; add herbs, nutmeg, and cheese, whisking until cheese is melted. Season to taste with salt, cayenne, and white pepper.

3. Pour sauce over turkey and broccoli in baking dish; sprinkle with breadcrumbs. Bake at 350° until bubbly, about 25 minutes.

Nutritional Data

PER SERVING		EXCHANGES	
Calories:	300	Milk:	0.5
% Calories from fat:	13	Vegetable:	1.0
Fat (gm):	4.2	Fruit:	0.0
Sat. fat (gm):	0.9	Bread:	1.0
Cholesterol (mg):	70.9	Meat:	3.0
Sodium (mg):	566	Fat:	0.0
Protein (gm):	37.4		
Carbohydrate (gm):	22.9		

TURKEY POT PIE

So tasty, you never realized Mom was disguising the leftovers from Thanksgiving dinner! Vary the vegetables for this versatile dish according to your family's preferences.

6 Servings

    Vegetable cooking spray
1 cup chopped onion
1/2 cup chopped green bell pepper
2 1/2 cups reduced-sodium chicken broth
1 cup cubed potato, turnip, *or* parsnip
1 cup sliced carrot
1 cup broccoli florets
3/4 cup small mushrooms
1/2 cup frozen whole-kernel corn
1/2 cup frozen peas
1 pound cooked, skinless turkey breast, cubed
1/2–3/4 teaspoon dried rosemary

    ¼ teaspoon dried thyme
    6 tablespoons all-purpose flour
    ½ cup fat-free half-and-half, *or* skim milk
       Salt and pepper, to taste
       Pot Pie Pastry (recipe follows)
       Skim milk, for brushing
    1 tablespoon grated Parmesan cheese

1. Spray large saucepan with cooking spray; heat over medium heat until hot. Saute onion and bell pepper until tender, about 5 minutes. Add chicken broth, remaining vegetables, turkey, and herbs. Heat to boiling; reduce heat and simmer, covered, until vegetables are tender, about 10 minutes.

2. Heat mixture to boiling. Mix flour and half-and-half; stir into boiling mixture. Boil, stirring constantly, until thickened, 1 to 2 minutes. Season to taste with salt and pepper. Pour into 2-quart casserole or soufflé dish.

3. Roll pastry on floured surface to fit top of casserole; place on casserole, trim, and flute. Cut steam vents in top of pastry. Bake at 425° for 20 minutes. Brush with skim milk and sprinkle with cheese; bake until golden, 5 to 10 minutes longer. Cool 5 to 10 minutes before serving.

Pot Pie Pastry

    1 cup all-purpose flour
    2 tablespoons grated Parmesan cheese
 2½–3 tablespoons vegetable shortening
  3–4 tablespoons ice water

1. Combine flour and Parmesan cheese in medium bowl. Cut in shortening with pastry blender until mixture resembles coarse crumbs. Add water, a tablespoon at a time, mixing with fork just until dough holds together. Refrigerate until ready to use.

Nutritional Data

PER SERVING		EXCHANGES	
Calories:	380	Milk:	0.0
% Calories from fat:	17	Vegetable:	0.0
Fat (gm):	7.1	Fruit:	0.0
Sat. fat (gm):	2.1	Bread:	3.0
Cholesterol (mg):	65.5	Meat:	3.0
Sodium (mg):	284	Fat:	0.0
Protein (gm):	32.8		
Carbohydrate (gm):	45.1		

4
FISH

Tuna Patties with Creamed Pea Sauce

Poached Salmon with Hollandaise Sauce

Flounder en Papillote

Shrimp De Jonghe

Seafood Newburg

TUNA PATTIES WITH CREAMED PEA SAUCE

◆

Canned tuna packed in water is much lower in fat than canned salmon. Serve these generous patties in buns, or pack the mixture into a small loaf pan and bake as a loaf.

4 Servings

- 2 cans (6 1/8 ounces each) light tuna packed in water, drained
- 3/4 cup dry unseasoned breadcrumbs, divided
- 1/4 cup finely chopped onion
- 1/4 cup finely chopped celery
- 2 tablespoons chopped red, *or* green bell, pepper
- 2–3 tablespoons fat-free mayonnaise
- 1–2 teaspoons Worcestershire sauce
  Salt and cayenne, to taste
- 1 egg
  Vegetable cooking spray
  Creamed Pea Sauce (recipe follows)

1. Combine tuna, 1/2 cup breadcrumbs, onion, celery, bell pepper, mayonnaise, and Worcestershire sauce in medium bowl; season to taste with salt and cayenne. Add egg, mixing until ingredients are well blended. Shape into 4 patties, each a generous 1/2 inch thick.

2. Spray a large skillet with cooking spray; heat over medium heat until hot. Coat patties with remaining 1/4 cup breadcrumbs; spray patties lightly with cooking spray. Cook over medium-low heat until browned, about 5 minutes on each side. Serve with Creamed Pea Sauce.

Creamed Pea Sauce

Makes about 1 cup

- 2 tablespoons margarine
- 2 tablespoons flour
- 1/2 cup skim milk
- 1/2 cup fat-free half-and-half, *or* skim milk
- 1/2 cup frozen, thawed peas
  Salt and pepper, to taste

1. Melt margarine in small saucepan. Stir in flour and cook, stirring constantly, over medium-low heat 1 minute. Whisk in milk and half-and-

half; heat to boiling. Boil, whisking constantly, until thickened, about 1 minute. Stir in peas; cook over low heat 2 to 3 minutes. Season to taste with salt and pepper. Serve hot.

Nutritional Data

PER SERVING		EXCHANGES	
Calories:	325	Milk:	0.5
% Calories from fat:	25	Vegetable:	1.0
Fat (gm):	8.9	Fruit:	0.0
Sat. fat (gm):	2	Bread:	1.0
Cholesterol (mg):	79.2	Meat:	3.5
Sodium (mg):	726	Fat:	0.0
Protein (gm):	30		
Carbohydrate (gm):	28.6		

POACHED SALMON WITH HOLLANDAISE SAUCE

This delicious offering can be served warm or cold depending upon the occasion and the season of the year.

6 Servings

3/4 cup dry white wine
1/2 cup water
2 thin slices onion
4 dill, or parsley, sprigs
1/4 teaspoon dried thyme
1/4 teaspoon dried tarragon
4 peppercorns
1 bay leaf
1/2 teaspoon salt
4 small salmon steaks (3 1/2–4 ounces each)
Mock Hollandaise Sauce (see p. 64)
Finely chopped parsley leaves, as garnish
4 lemon wedges, as garnish

1. Heat wine, water, onion, herbs, and salt to boiling in medium skillet. Reduce heat and simmer, covered, 5 minutes.

2. Add salmon to skillet; simmer, covered, until fish is cooked and flakes with a fork, 6 to 10 minutes, depending upon thickness of fish. Carefully remove fish from skillet with slotted pancake turner.

3. Arrange salmon on serving platter and spoon Hollandaise Sauce over; sprinkle with parsley. Serve with lemon wedges.

Nutritional Data

PER SERVING		EXCHANGES	
Calories:	195	Milk:	0.5
% Calories from fat:	30	Vegetable:	0.0
Fat (gm):	6.2	Fruit:	0.0
Sat. fat (gm):	0.9	Bread:	0.0
Cholesterol (mg):	53.3	Meat:	3.0
Sodium (mg):	351	Fat:	0.0
Protein (gm):	26.9		
Carbohydrate (gm):	4.2		

FLOUNDER EN PAPILLOTE

A lovely presentation, yet very simple to prepare.
Traditionally made with a lean white fish, you may want
to try the recipe with another fish, such as salmon or tuna.

6 Servings

  6 flounder, sole, or other lean white fish
      fillets (1½ pounds)
      Salt and pepper, to taste
  1 cup julienned, *or* shredded, carrot
  1 cup sliced mushrooms
  ¼ cup finely chopped shallot, *or* onion
  2 cloves garlic, minced
  ½ teaspoon dried tarragon
  2 teaspoons margarine
  ½ cup dry white wine, *or* water
  ¼ cup finely chopped parsley leaves
  6 lemon wedges

1. Cut out six 12-inch squares of parchment or microwave cooking paper. Fold each square in half, and cut each into a large heart shape. Open hearts and place 1 fish fillet on each; season lightly with salt and pepper.

2. Saute carrot, mushrooms, shallot, garlic, and tarragon in margarine in large skillet until carrots are crisp-tender, about 5 minutes. Stir in wine and parsley; season to taste with salt and pepper.

3. Spoon vegetable mixture over fish. Fold heart packets vertically, bringing edges together. Crimp edges to seal tightly. Place packets on jelly roll pan, and bake at 425° until packets puff, 10 to 12 minutes. Serve with lemon wedges.

Note

Aluminum foil can be used in place of cooking paper; bake fish about 5 minutes longer (packets will not puff when made with foil).

Nutritional Data

PER SERVING		EXCHANGES	
Calories:	149	Milk:	0.0
% Calories from fat:	17	Vegetable:	1.0
Fat (gm):	2.8	Fruit:	0.0
Sat. fat (gm):	0.6	Bread:	0.0
Cholesterol (mg):	59.8	Meat:	2.5
Sodium (mg):	118	Fat:	0.0
Protein (gm):	22.3		
Carbohydrate (gm):	5.7		

SHRIMP DE JONGHE

*For an elegant presentation, assemble and bake
the shrimp in individual shell dishes.*

4 Servings

 2 tablespoons finely chopped shallot, *or* onion
 4 cloves garlic, minced
 3 tablespoons margarine
 2 tablespoons dry sherry
 1 tablespoon lemon juice
 1/4 teaspoon dried marjoram
 1/4 teaspoon dried tarragon
   Pinch ground nutmeg
   Pinch cayenne
 1 cup fresh white breadcrumbs
 1/4 cup finely chopped parsley leaves
   Salt and pepper, to taste
 1 pound shrimp, peeled, deveined
 3 cups cooked rice

1. Saute shallot and garlic in margarine in medium skillet until tender, 2 to 3 minutes. Stir in sherry, lemon juice, marjoram, tarragon, nutmeg, and cayenne. Pour mixture over combined breadcrumbs and parsley in bowl and toss. Season to taste with salt and pepper.

2. Arrange shrimp in single layer on shell dishes or in 10 x 7-inch baking dish; top with crumb mixture. Bake at 450° until shrimp are cooked, about 10 minutes. Serve with rice.

Nutritional Data

PER SERVING		EXCHANGES	
Calories:	370	Milk:	0.0
% Calories from fat:	27	Vegetable:	1.0
Fat (gm):	10.8	Fruit:	0.0
Sat. fat (gm):	2.1	Bread:	2.5
Cholesterol (mg):	129.1	Meat:	2.0
Sodium (mg):	287	Fat:	1.0
Protein (gm):	22		
Carbohydrate (gm):	42.8		

SEAFOOD NEWBURG

Any shellfish or lean white fish can be used in this classic Newburg.

4 Servings

8 ounces shrimp, peeled, deveined
8 ounces bay scallops
1/2 cup water
1/4 cup finely chopped shallot, *or* onion
2 tablespoons margarine
1/4 cup all-purpose flour
1 1/2 cups fat-free half-and-half, *or* skim milk
1 egg yolk
1–2 tablespoons dry sherry
Pinch ground nutmeg
Pinch cayenne
Salt and white pepper, to taste
4 slices toast, cut diagonally into halves
Finely chopped parsley leaves, as garnish

1. Simmer shrimp and scallops in 1/2 cup water in small saucepan, covered, until cooked, 3 to 5 minutes. Drain, reserving liquid.

2. Saute shallot in margarine in medium saucepan until tender, 2 to 3 minutes. Mix in flour and cook 1 to 2 minutes. Whisk in half-and-half and reserved cooking liquid; heat to boiling. Boil, whisking constantly, until thickened, about 1 minute. Whisk about half the mixture into egg yolk in small bowl; whisk egg mixture back into saucepan. Cook over very low heat, whisking constantly, 30 seconds.

3. Stir in shrimp, scallops, sherry, nutmeg, and cayenne pepper; cook 2 to 3 minutes. Season to taste with salt and white pepper.

4. Arrange toast points on serving plates; spoon mixture over and sprinkle with parsley.

Nutritional Data

PER SERVING		EXCHANGES	
Calories:	326	Milk:	0.8
% Calories from fat:	26	Vegetable:	0.0
Fat (gm):	9.1	Fruit:	0.0
Sat. fat (gm):	1.8	Bread:	2.0
Cholesterol (mg):	164.8	Meat:	3.0
Sodium (mg):	495	Fat:	0.5
Protein (gm):	26.7		
Carbohydrate (gm):	29.9		

5
PASTA

Macaroni and Cheese

Turkey Tetrazzini

Spaghetti and Meatballs

Linguine with White Clam Sauce

Italian Lasagne

MACARONI AND CHEESE

For kids of all ages—always a favorite.

4 Servings (about 1 cup each)

¼ cup finely chopped onion
2 tablespoons margarine
¼ cup all-purpose flour
2½ cups skim milk
1 bay leaf
2 ounces light pasteurized processed cheese product, cubed
½ cup (2 ounces) shredded reduced-fat sharp, *or* mild, Cheddar cheese
1 teaspoon Dijon-style mustard
2 cups (10 ounces) elbow macaroni, cooked per package directions
Salt and cayenne, to taste
¼ teaspoon white pepper
2 tablespoons dry unseasoned breadcrumbs
Paprika, as garnish

1. Saute onion in margarine in medium saucepan until tender, 3 to 4 minutes. Stir in flour; cook over medium-low heat 1 minute, stirring constantly. Whisk in milk and bay leaf; heat to boiling. Boil, whisking constantly, until thickened, about 1 minute.

2. Stir in cheeses and mustard; cook over low heat, stirring constantly, until melted. Discard bay leaf.

3. Combine sauce and macaroni in 2-quart casserole. Season to taste with salt, cayenne, and white pepper; sprinkle with breadcrumbs and paprika. Bake, uncovered, at 350° until bubbly, 30 to 40 minutes.

Note

Any shape pasta, such as rotini, fusilli, or orrechiette, can be substituted for the macaroni.

Variations

Quick Mac 'n Cheese: Make recipe as above, but do not bake.

Macaroni and Cheese Primavera: Stir 1 cup cooked broccoli florets, 1 cup sauted sliced mushrooms, and ¼ cup sauteed chopped red bell pepper into the macaroni and sauce mixture in step 3; bake as above.

Nutritional Data

PER SERVING		EXCHANGES	
Calories:	495	Milk:	0.5
% Calories from fat:	21	Vegetable:	0.0
Fat (gm):	11.6	Fruit:	0.0
Sat. fat (gm):	3.6	Bread:	5.0
Cholesterol (mg):	17.7	Meat:	1.0
Sodium (mg):	577	Fat:	1.0
Protein (gm):	22		
Carbohydrate (gm):	73.9		

TURKEY TETRAZZINI

A favorite of the famous Italian opera singer,
Lucia Tetrazzini, for whom this famous comfort food was named.

8 Servings

- 8 ounces mushrooms, sliced
- 2 tablespoons margarine
- 2 tablespoons flour
- 1 can (14½ ounces) reduced-sodium chicken broth
- 1 cup skim milk
- ½ cup dry white wine, *or* skim milk
- 16 ounces thin, *or* regular, spaghetti, cooked per package directions
- 12 ounces cooked, cubed turkey, *or* chicken, breast
- ¼ cup grated Parmesan cheese
- ¼ teaspoon ground nutmeg
- ¼ teaspoon salt
- ¼ teaspoon pepper

1. Saute mushrooms in margarine in large saucepan until tender, about 5 minutes. Stir in flour; cook over medium heat 1 to 2 minutes more. Stir in chicken broth, milk, and wine and heat to boiling. Boil, stirring constantly, until thickened, 1 to 2 minutes (sauce will be very thin). Stir in pasta, turkey, Parmesan cheese, nutmeg, salt, and pepper.

2. Spoon pasta mixture into 2-quart casserole or baking dish. Bake, uncovered, at 350° until lightly browned and bubbly, about 45 minutes.

Nutritional Data

PER SERVING		EXCHANGES	
Calories:	370	Milk:	0.0
% Calories from fat:	16	Vegetable:	1.0
Fat (gm):	6.5	Fruit:	0.0
Sat. fat (gm):	1.7	Bread:	3.0
Cholesterol (mg):	35.7	Meat:	2.0
Sodium (mg):	218	Fat:	0.5
Protein (gm):	23.6		
Carbohydrate (gm):	50.3		

SPAGHETTI AND MEATBALLS

◆

*Use a small ice cream scoop to make the
meatballs—quick and easy!*

6 Servings

1 cup chopped onion
3 cloves garlic, minced
1 tablespoon olive oil
1 can (16 ounces) reduced-sodium whole
  tomatoes, drained, chopped
1 can (8 ounces) reduced-sodium tomato sauce
1 tablespoon tomato paste
1 teaspoon dried basil
1/2 teaspoon dried tarragon
1/2 teaspoon dried oregano
1/8 teaspoon crushed red pepper
1/2 teaspoon salt
1/4 teaspoon black pepper
  Meatballs (recipe follows)
12 ounces spaghetti, cooked per package
  directions

1. Saute onion and garlic in oil in large saucepan 2 to 3 minutes. Stir in tomatoes, tomato sauce, tomato paste, herbs, and red pepper; heat to boiling. Reduce heat and simmer, uncovered, 10 minutes; stir in salt and pepper.

2. Add Meatballs to sauce. Simmer, uncovered, until sauce is desired consistency, 10 to 15 minutes. Serve Meatballs and sauce over spaghetti.

Meatballs

Makes 18

1 pound 95% lean ground beef, *or* ground turkey
1/3 cup unseasoned dry breadcrumbs
1 egg white
3 cloves garlic, minced
3/4 teaspoon dried basil
3/4 teaspoon dried oregano
1/4 teaspoon dried thyme
1/2 teaspoon salt
1/4 teaspoon pepper
Vegetable cooking spray

1. Mix all ingredients; shape into 18 meatballs. Cook over medium heat in sprayed skillet until browned on all sides and no longer pink in the center, 8 to 10 minutes.

Nutritional Data

PER SERVING		EXCHANGES	
Calories:	439	Milk:	0.0
% Calories from fat:	15	Vegetable:	2.0
Fat (gm):	7.4	Fruit:	0.0
Sat. fat (gm):	1.9	Bread:	3.5
Cholesterol (mg):	43.3	Meat:	2.0
Sodium (mg):	493	Fat:	0.5
Protein (gm):	26.7		
Carbohydrate (gm):	65.2		

LINGUINE WITH WHITE CLAM SAUCE

Quick and easy to make, which is also a comfort!

4 Servings (about 1/2 cup sauce each)

3 cloves garlic, minced
1 tablespoon olive oil
2 tablespoons cornstarch
2 cups bottled clam juice
1/4 cup dry white wine, *or* water
1 pound drained fresh clams, *or* 2 cans (7½ ounces each) baby clams, undrained
1 tablespoon lemon juice
1 tablespoon finely chopped parsley leaves
1–2 teaspoons dried basil
1/8 teaspoon white pepper
8 ounces linguine, cooked per package directions, warm

1. Saute garlic in oil in medium saucepan 1 to 2 minutes. Mix cornstarch and clam juice; stir into saucepan. Stir in wine and heat to boiling; boil, stirring constantly, until thickened, about 1 minute.

2. Add clams and remaining ingredients, except linguine, to saucepan. Simmer, covered, until clams are cooked, 5 to 7 minutes. Serve over linguine.

Note

Many supermarkets sell fresh clams that are already shucked. If using clams in the shell, buy 2 to 3 dozen and see note following New England Clam Chowder (p. 6).

Nutritional Data

PER SERVING		EXCHANGES	
Calories:	319	Milk:	0.0
% Calories from fat:	18	Vegetable:	0.5
Fat (gm):	6.5	Fruit:	0.0
Sat. fat (gm):	0.6	Bread:	2.5
Cholesterol (mg):	38.6	Meat:	2.0
Sodium (mg):	305	Fat:	0.5
Protein (gm):	23.5		
Carbohydrate (gm):	39.1		

ITALIAN LASAGNE

The traditional lasagne we all remember, chock-full of Italian sausage and cheese but without excessive fat.

8 Servings

- 2 cups fat-free ricotta cheese
- 1/4 cup grated fat-free Parmesan cheese
- 3 cups (12 ounces) shredded, reduced-fat mozzarella cheese
  Herbed Tomato Sauce (recipe follows)
- 12 lasagna noodles, cooked per package directions
- 8 ounces reduced-fat turkey Italian sausage, cooked, well drained

1. Combine cheeses in bowl. Spread 1 cup tomato sauce on bottom of 13 x 9-inch baking pan; top with 4 lasagna noodles, overlapping to fit. Spoon 1/3 of cheese mixture over noodles, spreading lightly with rubber spatula. Top with 1 cup tomato sauce and half the sausage. Repeat layers 2 times, ending with layer of noodles, cheese, and tomato sauce.

2. Bake lasagne at 350°, loosely covered with aluminum foil, until bubbly, 50 to 60 minutes. Cool 10 minutes before cutting.

Herbed Tomato Sauce

Makes 4 1/2 cups

- Olive oil cooking spray
- 2 cups chopped onions
- 3 cloves garlic, minced
- 1 teaspoon dried basil
- 1 teaspoon dried tarragon
- 1 teaspoon dried thyme
- 2 cans (16 ounces each) reduced-sodium whole tomatoes, undrained, coarsely chopped
- 2 cans (8 ounces each) reduced-sodium tomato sauce
- 1 cup water
- 1–2 teaspoons sugar
- 1/4 teaspoon salt
- 1/4 teaspoon pepper

1. Spray large saucepan with cooking spray; heat over medium heat until hot. Saute onion and garlic until tender, about 5 minutes; stir in herbs and cook 1 to 2 minutes more.

2. Add tomatoes, tomato sauce, and water; heat to boiling. Reduce heat and simmer, uncovered, until sauce is reduced to about 4½ cups, 15 to 20 minutes. Stir in sugar, salt, and pepper.

Nutritional Data

PER SERVING		EXCHANGES	
Calories:	375	Milk:	0.0
% Calories from fat:	30	Vegetable:	2.5
Fat (gm):	12.9	Fruit:	0.0
Sat. fat (gm):	6	Bread:	1.5
Cholesterol (mg):	47.3	Meat:	3.5
Sodium (mg):	679	Fat:	0.5
Protein (gm):	31.3		
Carbohydrate (gm):	33.9		

6
CHEESE AND EGGS

Eggs Benedict

Quiche Lorraine

Welsh Rarebit

Cheddar Cheese Soufflé

Cheese Fondue

EGGS BENEDICT

+

*A hollandaise sauce that is almost too good to be
true brings a popular brunch dish back to the
table in healthy style. Six slices of English Muffin Bread
(see p. 109) can be substituted for the English muffins.*

(see p. 109)

6 Servings

6 ounces sliced lean Canadian bacon
3 English muffins, halved, toasted
6 poached eggs
   Mock Hollandaise Sauce (recipe follows)
   Paprika, as garnish
   Finely chopped parsley leaves, as garnish

1. Heat Canadian bacon in small skillet until hot and lightly browned.
Arrange Canadian bacon on muffin halves and top with poached eggs.

2. Spoon Mock Hollandaise Sauce over eggs; sprinkle with paprika and
parsley.

Mock Hollandaise Sauce

Makes about 1 1/2 cups

6 ounces fat-free cream cheese
1/3 cup fat-free sour cream
3–4 tablespoons skim milk
1–2 teaspoons lemon juice
1/2–1 teaspoon Dijon-style mustard
1/8 teaspoon ground turmeric

1. Heat all ingredients in small saucepan over medium-low to low heat
until melted and smooth, stirring constantly. Serve immediately.

Nutritional Data

PER SERVING		EXCHANGES	
Calories:	204	Milk:	0.0
% Calories from fat:	27	Vegetable:	0.0
Fat (gm):	5.6	Fruit:	0.0
Sat. fat (gm):	1.7	Bread:	1.0
Cholesterol (mg):	228.3	Meat:	2.5
Sodium (mg):	786	Fat:	0.0
Protein (gm):	19		
Carbohydrate (gm):	17		

QUICHE LORRAINE

Enjoy the rich texture and flavor of this classic quiche, modified to low-fat goodness by using a combination of skim and evaporated skim milk. For Spinach Quiche, see the variation following the recipe.

6 Servings

Reduced-Fat Pie Pastry (recipe follows)
Vegetable cooking spray
1/4 cup finely chopped onion
3/4 cup skim milk
1/2 can (12-ounce size) evaporated skim milk
1 egg
2 egg whites
1/4 cup fat-free sour cream
1/4 teaspoon salt
1/8 teaspoon cayenne
1/8 teaspoon ground nutmeg
1 cup (4 ounces) shredded fat-free Swiss cheese
1 tablespoon flour
2 slices bacon, cooked, well drained, crumbled

1. Roll pastry on floured surface into circle 1 inch larger than inverted 8-inch pie pan. Ease pastry into pan; trim and flute. Line bottom of pastry with aluminum foil and fill with a single layer of pie weights or dried beans. Bake at 425° for 7 minutes; remove pie weights and foil. Bake 3 to 5 minutes longer or until crust is light golden brown. Cool on wire rack.

2. Spray small skillet with cooking spray; place over medium heat until hot. Saute onion until tender, 3 to 5 minutes.

3. Mix skim and evaporated skim milk, eggs, egg whites, sour cream, salt, cayenne, and nutmeg in medium bowl until smooth. Toss cheese with flour; stir into milk mixture. Stir in bacon and onion and pour into baked pie crust.

4. Bake quiche at 350° until set in the center, and a sharp knife inserted near center comes out clean, about 40 minutes. Cover edge of pie crust with aluminum foil if becoming too brown. Cool quiche on wire rack 5 minutes before cutting.

Reduced-Fat Pie Pastry

For one 9-inch pie

1¼ cups all-purpose flour
¼ teaspoon salt
3 tablespoons margarine, *or* vegetable
    shortening
3–4 tablespoons ice water

1. Combine flour and salt in medium bowl; cut in margarine with pastry blender until mixture forms coarse crumbs. Sprinkle with ice water, 1 tablespoon at a time, mixing with fork until dough holds together. Refrigerate, covered, 30 minutes before using.

Variation

Spinach Quiche: Replace step 2 as follows: spray medium skillet with vegetable cooking spray; place over medium heat until hot. Saute ¼ cup finely chopped onion until tender, 3 to 5 minutes. Drain ½ package (10-ounce size) frozen thawed spinach between paper toweling. Add spinach to skillet, cooking over medium to medium-low heat until mixture is quite dry, 3 to 4 minutes. Stir spinach mixture (instead of onion) into milk mixture in step 3 and proceed as above.

Nutritional Data

PER SERVING		EXCHANGES	
Calories:	249	Milk:	0.5
% Calories from fat:	29	Vegetable:	0.0
Fat (gm):	7.9	Fruit:	0.0
Sat. fat (gm):	1.9	Bread:	1.5
Cholesterol (mg):	38.7	Meat:	1.0
Sodium (mg):	611	Fat:	1.0
Protein (gm):	14.1		
Carbohydrate (gm):	29.2		

WELSH RAREBIT

Perhaps you know this dish as Welsh Rabbit. Whatever the name, the distinctively flavored sauce is rich and delicious.

6 Servings (about 1/2 cup sauce each)

- 1/4 cup very finely chopped onion
- 2 tablespoons margarine
- 1/4 cup all-purpose flour
- 2 cups skim milk
- 1/2 cup white wine, *or* skim milk
- 2 ounces light pasteurized processed cheese product, cubed
- 1/2 cup (2 ounces) reduced-fat sharp Cheddar cheese
- 1/4–1/2 teaspoon dry mustard
- 1/2 teaspoon Worcestershire sauce
- White and cayenne pepper, to taste
- 6 slices sourdough, *or* multigrain, bread
- Butter-flavor vegetable cooking spray
- 1 large ripe tomato, cut into 6 slices
- Finely chopped parsley leaves, as garnish

1. Saute onion in margarine in medium saucepan until tender, 2 to 3 minutes. Stir in flour and cook over medium-low heat, stirring constantly, 1 minute. Whisk in milk and wine; heat to boiling. Boil, whisking constantly, until thickened, about 1 minute.

2. Stir in cheeses, dry mustard, and Worcestershire sauce; cook over low heat until cheeses are melted. Season to taste with white and cayenne pepper.

3. Spray both sides of bread with cooking spray; cook over medium heat in large skillet until browned, 2 to 3 minutes on each side. Broil tomato slices 4 inches from heat source until hot through. Arrange bread on plates; top with tomato slices, and spoon cheese sauce over. Sprinkle with parsley.

Notes

Regular toast can be used instead of pan-grilling the bread in step 3.

Cheese Rarebit is also delicious served over sliced ham or chicken breast and asparagus spears on toast.

Nutritional Data

PER SERVING		EXCHANGES	
Calories:	219	Milk:	0.0
% Calories from fat:	31	Vegetable:	0.0
Fat (gm):	7.6	Fruit:	0.0
Sat. fat (gm):	2.4	Bread:	1.5
Cholesterol (mg):	11.5	Meat:	1.0
Sodium (mg):	502	Fat:	1.0
Protein (gm):	9.9		
Carbohydrate (gm):	24.1		

CHEDDAR CHEESE SOUFFLÉ

This spectacular soufflé soars above the soufflé dish!

4 Servings

Vegetable cooking spray
1–2 tablespoons grated fat-free Parmesan cheese
1 cup skim milk
3 tablespoons flour
$1/2$ teaspoon dry mustard
$1/2$ teaspoon snipped fresh chives
$1/2$ teaspoon dried marjoram
$1/4$ teaspoon cayenne
1–2 pinches ground nutmeg
3 egg yolks
$1^1/4$ cups (5 ounces) shredded fat-free Cheddar cheese
Salt and white pepper, to taste
3 egg whites
$1/4$ teaspoon cream of tartar

1. Spray 1-quart soufflé dish with cooking spray and coat with Parmesan cheese. Attach an aluminum foil collar to dish, extending foil 3 inches above top of dish; spray inside of collar with cooking spray.

2. Mix milk and flour until smooth in small saucepan; mix in mustard, chives, marjoram, cayenne, and nutmeg. Heat to boiling, whisking constantly; boil until thickened, about 1 minute, whisking constantly.

3. To egg yolks in small bowl, whisk in about $1/2$ cup milk mixture. Whisk egg mixture back into saucepan. Add cheese; cook over low heat until melted. Season to taste with salt and white pepper.

4. Beat egg whites until foamy; add cream of tartar and beat to stiff, but not dry, peaks. Stir about ⅓ of egg whites into cheese mixture; fold cheese mixture into remaining whites. Spoon into prepared soufflé dish. Bake at 350° until soufflé is puffed, browned, and just set in the center, 35 to 40 minutes. Serve immediately.

Nutritional Data

PER SERVING		EXCHANGES	
Calories:	162	Milk:	0.0
% Calories from fat:	23	Vegetable:	0.0
Fat (gm):	4.1	Fruit:	0.0
Sat. fat (gm):	1.3	Bread:	0.5
Cholesterol (mg):	160.8	Meat:	2.5
Sodium (mg):	340	Fat:	0.0
Protein (gm):	19.3		
Carbohydrate (gm):	11.2		

CHEESE FONDUE

Flavorful with wine and a hint of garlic, this creamy fondue is made entirely with fat-free cheese!

8 Servings (¼ cup fondue each)

1½ cups dry white wine
2–3 large cloves garlic, peeled
1 package (8 ounces) fat-free cream cheese
2 cups (8 ounces) shredded fat-free Swiss cheese
1 tablespoon flour
Salt, cayenne, and black pepper, to taste
French or Italian bread, cubed, for dipping (optional)

1. Heat wine and garlic cloves to boiling in medium saucepan; reduce heat and boil gently until reduced to ¾ cup. Discard garlic.

2. Add cream cheese and cook over low heat, stirring until melted and smooth. Toss shredded cheese with flour; add to saucepan and cook, stirring constantly, until melted. Season to taste with salt, cayenne, and black pepper.

3. Serve in fondue pot or bowl with bread cubes for dipping.

Notes

Instead of wine, ¾ cup skim milk can be substituted. Simmer with garlic 5 minutes, then proceed with recipe as above.

If fondue becomes too thick, it can be thinned with white wine, skim milk, or water.

Nutritional Data

PER SERVING		EXCHANGES	
Calories:	100	Milk:	0.0
% Calories from fat:	0	Vegetable:	0.0
Fat (gm):	0	Fruit:	0.0
Sat. fat (gm):	0	Bread:	0.0
Cholesterol (mg):	0	Meat:	1.5
Sodium (mg):	547	Fat:	0.0
Protein (gm):	10.9		
Carbohydrate (gm):	5		

7
VEGETABLES

Artichokes with Hollandaise Sauce

Green Bean Casserole

New England Baked Beans

Harvard Beets

Cauliflower with Creamy Cheese Sauce

Corn Pudding

Real Mashed Potatoes

Potatoes Gratin

Twice-Baked Potatoes with Cheese

Crispy Fries

Creamed Spinach

Tomato Pudding

Candied Yams

ARTICHOKES WITH HOLLANDAISE SAUCE

The Hollandaise Sauce is excellent served over steamed asparagus spears or broccoli. Also, see our recipe for Poached Salmon with Hollandaise Sauce (see p. 50).

4 to 6 Servings

4–6 whole artichokes, stems trimmed
Mock Hollandaise Sauce (see p. 64)

1. Slice 1 inch off tops of artichokes and discard. Trim tips of remaining leaves with scissors. Place artichokes in medium saucepan with 2 inches of water; heat to boiling. Reduce heat and simmer, covered, until artichoke leaves pull off easily and bottom is tender when pierced with a fork, about 30 minutes.

2. Place artichokes on serving plates with Hollandaise Sauce on the side for dipping.

Nutritional Data

PER SERVING		EXCHANGES	
Calories:	114	Milk:	0.5
% Calories from fat:	2	Vegetable:	2.0
Fat (gm):	0.3	Fruit:	0.0
Sat. fat (gm):	0.1	Bread:	0.0
Cholesterol (mg):	0.2	Meat:	0.5
Sodium (mg):	396	Fat:	0.0
Protein (gm):	11.9		
Carbohydrate (gm):	17.5		

GREEN BEAN CASSEROLE

Reduced-fat cream of mushroom soup and fat-free sour cream make this old favorite possible in a new skinny form. We've used fresh green beans, but canned or frozen may be used if you prefer.

6 Servings

- 1 can (10³/₄ ounces) reduced-fat cream of mushroom soup
- ¹/₂ cup fat-free sour cream
- ¹/₄ cup skim milk
- 1¹/₄ pounds green beans, cut into 1¹/₂-inch pieces, cooked until crisp-tender
- ¹/₂ cup canned French-fried onions

1. Mix soup, sour cream, and milk in 2-quart casserole; stir in beans.

2. Bake, uncovered, at 350° until mixture is bubbly, about 45 minutes. Sprinkle onions on top during last 5 minutes of baking time.

Nutritional Data

PER SERVING		EXCHANGES	
Calories:	81	Milk:	0.0
% Calories from fat:	31	Vegetable:	2.0
Fat (gm):	2.9	Fruit:	0.0
Sat. fat (gm):	0.8	Bread:	0.0
Cholesterol (mg):	1.3	Meat:	0.0
Sodium (mg):	172	Fat:	0.5
Protein (gm):	3		
Carbohydrate (gm):	11.6		

NEW ENGLAND BAKED BEANS

Long-baked and savory, these beans are the best!
Bacon replaces the higher-fat salt pork traditionally
used in the recipe. If you prefer soaking beans
overnight, delete step 1 and proceed with step 2.

8 to 10 Servings (about $^{1}/_{2}$ cup each)

8 ounces dried navy, *or* Great Northern, beans, washed, sorted
 Water
4 slices bacon, fried crisp, well drained, cut into 1-inch pieces
$^{3}/_{4}$ cup chopped onion
1 clove garlic
3 tablespoons tomato paste
3 tablespoons dark molasses
3 tablespoons packed light brown sugar
$^{1}/_{2}$ teaspoon dry mustard
$^{1}/_{4}$ teaspoon dried thyme
$^{1}/_{2}$ teaspoon salt

1. Cover beans with 2 inches of water in large saucepan; heat to boiling and boil, uncovered, 2 minutes. Remove from heat and let stand, covered, 1 hour.

2. Add more water to beans to cover, if necessary. Heat to boiling; reduce heat and simmer, covered, until beans are tender, about 1$^{1}/_{4}$ hours. Drain beans; reserve liquid.

3. Mix beans, bacon, onion, garlic, tomato paste, molasses, brown sugar, dry mustard, thyme, and salt in 1$^{1}/_{2}$-quart casserole; add enough reserved cooking liquid to cover beans. Bake, covered, at 325°, stirring occasionally, 3 hours. Bake, uncovered, until beans are desired consistency, about 1 hour more.

Nutritional Data

PER SERVING		EXCHANGES	
Calories:	161	Milk:	0.0
% Calories from fat:	11	Vegetable:	0.0
Fat (gm):	2.1	Fruit:	0.0
Sat. fat (gm):	0.7	Bread:	2.0
Cholesterol (mg):	2.7	Meat:	0.0
Sodium (mg):	246	Fat:	0.5
Protein (gm):	7.8		
Carbohydrate (gm):	29.1		

HARVARD BEETS

Sweet yet tart, the sauce can also be served over cooked carrots or pearl onions. Vary the amount of vinegar for the tartness you like.

4 Servings

    3 tablespoons sugar
 1½ tablespoons cornstarch
  ¾ cup water
 3–4 tablespoons cider vinegar
    2 teaspoons margarine
      Salt and white pepper, to taste
    1 pound beets, cooked, sliced or julienned,
      warm

1. Mix sugar and cornstarch in small saucepan; whisk in water and vinegar. Heat to boiling, whisking constantly; boil, whisking constantly, until thickened, about 1 minute. Add margarine, whisking until melted. Season to taste with salt and pepper.

2. Pour sauce over beets in serving bowl and toss gently.

Nutritional Data

PER SERVING		EXCHANGES	
Calories:	94	Milk:	0.0
% Calories from fat:	18	Vegetable:	2.0
Fat (gm):	1.9	Fruit:	0.0
Sat. fat (gm):	0.4	Bread:	0.5
Cholesterol (mg):	0	Meat:	0.0
Sodium (mg):	70	Fat:	0.0
Protein (gm):	1.1		
Carbohydrate (gm):	19.3		

CAULIFLOWER WITH CREAMY CHEESE SAUCE

Try making the cheese sauce with other reduced-fat cheeses, such as Havarti, Gruyère, American, or blue, for new flavor variations.

6 Servings

1 whole cauliflower (2 pounds)
   Creamy Cheese Sauce (recipe follows)
   Paprika, as garnish
   Finely chopped parsley leaves, as garnish

1. Place cauliflower in saucepan with 2 inches of water; heat to boiling. Reduce heat and simmer, covered, until cauliflower is tender, 20 to 25 minutes.

2. Place cauliflower on serving plate; spoon Creamy Cheese Sauce over and sprinkle with paprika and parsley.

Creamy Cheese Sauce

Makes about 1¹/₄ cups

2 tablespoons minced onion
1 tablespoon margarine
2 tablespoons flour
1 cup skim milk
¹/₂ cup (2 ounces) cubed reduced-fat pasteurized processed cheese product, *or* shredded reduced-fat Cheddar cheese
¹/₄ teaspoon dry mustard
2–3 drops red pepper sauce
   Salt and white pepper, to taste

1. Saute onion in margarine in small saucepan 2 to 3 minutes. Stir in flour; cook over medium-low heat, stirring constantly, 1 minute. Whisk in milk and heat to boiling; boil, whisking constantly, until thickened, about 1 minute.

2. Reduce heat to low. Add cheese, dry mustard, and pepper sauce, whisking until cheese is melted. Season to taste with salt and pepper.

Nutritional Data

PER SERVING		EXCHANGES	
Calories:	102	Milk:	0.0
% Calories from fat:	31	Vegetable:	2.0
Fat (gm):	3.6	Fruit:	0.0
Sat. fat (gm):	1.5	Bread:	0.0
Cholesterol (mg):	5.7	Meat:	0.5
Sodium (mg):	194	Fat:	0.5
Protein (gm):	6.5		
Carbohydrate (gm):	11.7		

CORN PUDDING

◆

Cut fresh corn from the cob for best flavor, though frozen corn can be used for convenience.

6 Servings

Vegetable cooking spray
2 tablespoons plain dry breadcrumbs
2 cups fresh, *or* frozen, and thawed, whole-kernel corn
1/2 cup skim milk
3 tablespoons flour
1 1/2 tablespoons margarine, softened
1 egg
2 egg whites
1 teaspoon sugar
1/2 teaspoon dried thyme
1/2 teaspoon salt
1/8 teaspoon pepper

1. Spray 1-quart casserole or soufflé dish with cooking spray; coat dish with breadcrumbs.

2. Process corn, milk, and flour in food processor or blender until a coarse puree. Beat margarine, egg, and egg whites in medium bowl until smooth; mix in sugar, thyme, salt, and pepper. Stir in corn mixture, and pour into prepared casserole.

3. Bake, uncovered, at 350° until pudding is set and beginning to brown, about 35 minutes. Serve warm.

Nutritional Data

PER SERVING
		EXCHANGES	
Calories:	122	Milk:	0.0
% Calories from fat:	28	Vegetable:	0.0
Fat (gm):	3.9	Fruit:	0.0
Sat. fat (gm):	0.9	Bread:	1.0
Cholesterol (mg):	35.8	Meat:	0.5
Sodium (mg):	272	Fat:	0.5
Protein (gm):	5.3		
Carbohydrate (gm):	17.9		

REAL MASHED POTATOES

Just like grandma used to make! For a country-style variation, leave potatoes unpeeled.

6 Servings (about ²/₃ cup each)

2 pounds Idaho potatoes, peeled, quartered, cooked until tender
¹/₂ cup fat-free sour cream
¹/₄ cup skim milk, hot
2 tablespoons margarine
Salt and pepper, to taste

1. Mash potatoes, or beat until smooth, in medium bowl, adding sour cream, milk, and margarine. Season to taste with salt and pepper.

Variations

Garlic Mashed Potatoes: Cook 10 peeled cloves of garlic with the potatoes. Follow recipe above, mashing garlic with potatoes.

Horseradish Mashed Potatoes: Make Real or Garlic Mashed Potatoes, beating in 2 teaspoons horseradish.

Potato Pancakes: Make any of the mashed potato recipes above; refrigerate until chilled. Mix in 2 egg whites (or ¹/₄ cup real egg product), 4 chopped green onions and tops, and ¹/₄ cup fat-free grated Parmesan cheese (optional). Form mixture into 8 patties, using about ¹/₂ cup mixture for each. Coat patties in flour, dip in beaten egg white, and coat with plain dry breadcrumbs. Cook over medium-high heat in lightly greased large skillet until browned, 3 to 5 minutes on each side.

Nutritional Data

PER SERVING		EXCHANGES	
Calories:	165	Milk:	0.0
% Calories from fat:	21	Vegetable:	0.0
Fat (gm):	3.9	Fruit:	0.0
Sat. fat (gm):	0.8	Bread:	2.0
Cholesterol (mg):	0.2	Meat:	0.0
Sodium (mg):	70	Fat:	0.5
Protein (gm):	4.1		
Carbohydrate (gm):	29.6		

POTATOES GRATIN

These potatoes are so rich and creamy you'll never believe they were made without heavy cream!

8 Servings (about 1/2 cup each)

  2 tablespoons margarine
  3 tablespoons flour
1 3/4 cups skim milk
  2 ounces light pasteurized processed cheese product, cubed
  1/2 cup (2 ounces) shredded reduced-fat Cheddar cheese
     Salt and pepper, to taste
  2 pounds Idaho potatoes, peeled, cut into scant 1/4-inch slices
  1/4 cup very thinly sliced onion
     Ground nutmeg, to taste

1. Melt margarine in medium saucepan; stir in flour and cook over medium heat, stirring constantly, 2 minutes. Whisk in milk and heat to boiling; boil, stirring constantly, until thickened. Remove from heat; add cheeses, stirring until melted. Season to taste with salt and pepper.

2. Layer 1/3 of the potatoes and onion in bottom of 2-quart casserole; sprinkle lightly with salt, pepper, and nutmeg. Spoon 2/3 cup sauce over. Repeat layers 2 times, using remaining ingredients.

3. Bake, covered, at 350° for 45 minutes; uncover and bake until potatoes are fork-tender and browned, 20 to 30 minutes more.

Variations

Scalloped Potatoes: Make white sauce as above, increasing margarine to 3 tablespoons, flour to ¼ cup, and milk to 2¼ cups; delete cheeses. Assemble and bake as directed.

Scalloped Potatoes and Ham: Trim visible fat from 1 pound lean smoked ham; cut into cubes. Make Scalloped Potatoes as above, layering ham between potatoes.

Nutritional Data

PER SERVING		EXCHANGES	
Calories:	202	Milk:	0.0
% Calories from fat:	23	Vegetable:	0.0
Fat (gm):	5.1	Fruit:	0.0
Sat. fat (gm):	1.7	Bread:	2.0
Cholesterol (mg):	8.5	Meat:	0.5
Sodium (mg):	259	Fat:	0.5
Protein (gm):	7.6		
Carbohydrate (gm):	31.7		

TWICE-BAKED POTATOES WITH CHEESE

These stuffed bakers are the perfect accompaniment to Mock Chicken Legs or Just Plain Meat Loaf (see pp. 27, 22). The potatoes can be prepared and refrigerated 24 hours in advance; bake 5 to 10 minutes longer than indicated in recipe.

4 Servings

2 large Idaho potatoes (8 ounces each)
1/4 cup fat-free sour cream
1/4 cup skim milk
3/4 cup (3 ounces) shredded reduced-fat sharp, *or* mild, Cheddar cheese, divided
Salt and pepper, to taste
Paprika, as garnish

1. Pierce potatoes with a fork and bake at 400° until tender, about 1 hour. Cut into halves; let cool enough to handle.

2. Scoop out inside of potatoes, being careful to leave shells intact. Mash warm potatoes, or beat until smooth, in medium bowl, adding sour cream, milk, and 1/2 cup of cheese. Season to taste with salt and pepper.

3. Spoon potato mixture into potato shells; sprinkle with remaining 1/4 cup cheese and paprika. Bake at 400° until hot through, 15 to 20 minutes.

Nutritional Data

PER SERVING		EXCHANGES	
Calories:	177	Milk:	0.0
% Calories from fat:	16	Vegetable:	0.0
Fat (gm):	3.2	Fruit:	0.0
Sat. fat (gm):	1.6	Bread:	2.0
Cholesterol (mg):	11.6	Meat:	0.5
Sodium (mg):	314	Fat:	0.0
Protein (gm):	8.4		
Carbohydrate (gm):	29.2		

CRISPY FRIES

Golden brown, delicious, and crisp, these potatoes look and taste like they have been deep-fried—the secret is salting the raw potatoes!

4 to 6 Servings

1 pound Idaho potatoes, unpeeled
2 teaspoons salt
  Vegetable cooking spray
  Salt and pepper, to taste

1. Cut potatoes into sticks 3 to 4 inches long and a scant ½ inch wide. Sprinkle lightly with 2 teaspoons salt and let stand 10 minutes. Rinse potatoes in cold water and dry well on paper toweling.

2. Spray non-stick jelly roll pan with cooking spray. Arrange potatoes in single layer on pan; spray generously with cooking spray, tossing to coat all sides. Sprinkle potatoes lightly with salt and pepper.

3. Bake at 350° until potatoes are golden brown and crisp, 40 to 45 minutes, turning halfway through cooking time.

Note

Potatoes can be held in a 200° oven for up to 1 hour.

Variations

Parmesan Fries: Follow recipe, sprinkling potatoes lightly with fat-free grated Parmesan cheese before baking.

Steak Fries: Cut potatoes into wedges 4 inches long and 1 inch wide. Follow recipe as above, baking until golden brown and crisp, 1 to 1¼ hours.

Nutritional Data

PER SERVING		EXCHANGES	
Calories:	166	Milk:	0.0
% Calories from fat:	1	Vegetable:	0.0
Fat (gm):	0.2	Fruit:	0.0
Sat. fat (gm):	0	Bread:	2.5
Cholesterol (mg):	0	Meat:	0.0
Sodium (mg):	12	Fat:	0.0
Protein (gm):	3.5		
Carbohydrate (gm):	38.6		

CREAMED SPINACH

---◆---

For an au gratin version of this dish, mix spinach with all but ¼ cup of the sauce and spoon into a small casserole. Spoon ¼ cup of sauce over the top, and sprinkle with 2 to 3 tablespoons of grated Parmesan cheese or reduced-fat mild Cheddar cheese. Bake at 425° until cheese is melted, 2 to 3 minutes.

4 Servings

2 packages (10 ounces each) spinach, stems trimmed
¼ cup finely chopped onion
2 teaspoons margarine
2 tablespoons flour
1 cup skim milk, *or* fat-free half-and-half
¼ cup fat-free sour cream
   Ground nutmeg, to taste
   Salt and pepper, to taste

1. Rinse spinach and place in large saucepan with water clinging to leaves. Cook, covered, over medium-high heat until spinach is wilted, 3 to 4 minutes. Drain excess liquid.

2. Saute onion in margarine in small saucepan until tender, 3 to 5 minutes. Stir in flour; cook over medium-low heat 1 minute, stirring constantly. Whisk in milk; heat to boiling. Boil, whisking constantly, until thickened, about 1 minute. Remove from heat and stir in sour cream.

3. Pour sauce over spinach and mix lightly; season to taste with nutmeg, salt, and pepper.

Nutritional Data

PER SERVING		EXCHANGES	
Calories:	92	Milk:	0.0
% Calories from fat:	20	Vegetable:	2.5
Fat (gm):	2.2	Fruit:	0.0
Sat. fat (gm):	0.5	Bread:	0.0
Cholesterol (mg):	1	Meat:	0.0
Sodium (mg):	145	Fat:	0.5
Protein (gm):	6.6		
Carbohydrate (gm):	13.3		

TOMATO PUDDING

Do use a good quality, firm French, Italian, or sourdough bread for the croutons, as a soft bread will become too soft in baking.

4 Servings

1½ cups cubed firm bread, such as French or
Italian
Vegetable cooking spray
½ cup thinly sliced celery
½ cup chopped onion
½ cup chopped green bell pepper
1 can (16 ounces) reduced-sodium whole
tomatoes, undrained, coarsely chopped
½ teaspoon celery seed
½ teaspoon dried marjoram
1 tablespoon light brown sugar
Salt and pepper, to taste

1. Spray bread cubes generously with cooking spray; arrange in single layer in baking pan. Bake at 375° until browned, stirring occasionally, 8 to 10 minutes.

2. Spray medium skillet with cooking spray; heat over medium heat until hot. Saute celery, onion, and bell pepper until tender, about 8 minutes. Stir in tomatoes, celery seed, marjoram, and brown sugar and heat to boiling. Reduce heat and simmer, covered, 2 to 3 minutes. Pour mixture into 1-quart soufflé dish or casserole; season to taste with salt and pepper.

3. Stir croutons into tomato mixture, leaving some of the croutons on the top. Bake at 425° until hot through, about 20 minutes. Serve hot.

Notes

Dry "stuffing" cubes can be substituted for the croutons.

Two cups coarsely chopped fresh tomatoes can be substituted for the canned tomatoes; simmer as above until tomatoes wilt and release juices, 5 to 8 minutes.

Nutritional Data

PER SERVING		EXCHANGES	
Calories:	85	Milk:	0.0
% Calories from fat:	9	Vegetable:	2.0
Fat (gm):	0.9	Fruit:	0.0
Sat. fat (gm):	0.1	Bread:	0.5
Cholesterol (mg):	0	Meat:	0.0
Sodium (mg):	88	Fat:	0.0
Protein (gm):	2.6		
Carbohydrate (gm):	17.9		

CANDIED YAMS

◆

Whether called yams or sweet potatoes in your family, the sweet goodness of this dish is the same! If marshmallows are a must, add them 10 minutes before the end of baking time.

8 to 10 Servings

$^1/_3$ cup packed light brown sugar
2 tablespoons light corn syrup
1 tablespoon flour
1 tablespoon margarine
1 can (40 ounces) cut sweet potatoes in syrup, drained, sliced

1. Combine brown sugar, corn syrup, flour, and margarine in small saucepan; heat just to boiling, stirring constantly, and remove from heat.

2. Layer sweet potatoes in 10 x 6-inch baking dish, spooning glaze between each layer and over the top. Bake, uncovered, at 350° until hot, 25 to 30 minutes.

Note

Two pounds fresh sweet potatoes can be substituted for the canned. Peel and slice potatoes. Cook, covered, in medium saucepan in 2 to 3 inches of simmering water until fork-tender, about 10 minutes. Drain well, cool slightly, and proceed with step 2 as above.

Nutritional Data

PER SERVING		EXCHANGES	
Calories:	176	Milk:	0.0
% Calories from fat:	8	Vegetable:	0.0
Fat (gm):	1.5	Fruit:	0.0
Sat. fat (gm):	0.3	Bread:	2.5
Cholesterol (mg):	0	Meat:	0.0
Sodium (mg):	63	Fat:	0.0
Protein (gm):	1.5		
Carbohydrate (gm):	39.5		

8
SALADS

Perfection Salad

Frozen Fruit Salad

Carrot-Raisin Salad

Creamy Potato Salad

German Potato Salad

Macaroni Salad

Freezer Coleslaw

Waldorf Salad

Wilted Spinach Salad

Caesar Salad

Ten-Layer Salad

PERFECTION SALAD

This is my sister Nancy's favorite salad, and although she thinks it's "perfect," the true origin of the name is unclear. For quick and easy preparation, 2³/₄ cups of packaged coleslaw ingredients can be used.

12 Servings

 1 can (8 ounces) crushed pineapple in its own juice, undrained
 1 package (6 ounces) lemon, lime, or orange flavor gelatin
 ¹/₄ teaspoon salt
 1¹/₂ cups thinly sliced, *or* shredded, cabbage
 ¹/₂ cup chopped celery
 ¹/₂ cup shredded carrot
 ¹/₄ cup chopped red, *or* green bell, pepper
 ¹/₄–¹/₂ cup sliced pimiento-stuffed olives
  Lettuce leaves, as garnish
 ³/₄ cup fat-free mayonnaise

1. Drain pineapple, reserving juice. Prepare gelatin in large bowl according to package directions, adding salt and using reserved pineapple juice as part of the liquid.

2. Mix pineapple, cabbage, celery, carrot, bell pepper, and olives into gelatin mixture. Pour into ungreased 13 x 9-inch baking dish. Refrigerate until firm, 4 to 5 hours.

3. Cut salad into squares; arrange on lettuce-lined plates. Top each serving with a tablespoon of mayonnaise.

Nutritional Data

PER SERVING		EXCHANGES	
Calories:	69	Milk:	0.0
% Calories from fat:	6	Vegetable:	0.0
Fat (gm):	0.5	Fruit:	0.0
Sat. fat (gm):	0.1	Bread:	1.0
Cholesterol (mg):	0	Meat:	0.0
Sodium (mg):	346	Fat:	0.0
Protein (gm):	0.9		
Carbohydrate (gm):	15.1		

FROZEN FRUIT SALAD

So simple, but so very tasty—serve as a dessert too!

8 to 12 Servings

1 package (8 ounces) fat-free cream cheese
1 cup fat-free sour cream
$^1/_3$ cup sugar
1 tablespoon grated lemon rind
   Pinch salt
5 cups assorted fresh, frozen, or canned fruit
   (drained crushed pineapple, strawberries,
   blueberries, raspberries, cherries, peaches,
   etc.)
   Lettuce leaves, as garnish

1. Beat cream cheese, sour cream, sugar, lemon rind, and salt in large bowl until smooth. Mix in fruit. Spread in 10 x 6-inch baking dish and freeze until firm, 8 hours or overnight.

2. Let stand at room temperature until softened enough to cut, 10 to 15 minutes. Cut into squares and serve on lettuce-lined plates.

Nutritional Data

PER SERVING		EXCHANGES	
Calories:	126	Milk:	0.0
% Calories from fat:	2	Vegetable:	0.0
Fat (gm):	0.3	Fruit:	1.0
Sat. fat (gm):	0	Bread:	0.0
Cholesterol (mg):	0	Meat:	0.5
Sodium (mg):	191	Fat:	0.0
Protein (gm):	6.6		
Carbohydrate (gm):	25.2		

CARROT-RAISIN SALAD

Comfort salad at its best! A small can of drained pineapple tidbits can be added to the salad, if you like.

6 Servings (about 1/3 cup each)

2½ cups shredded carrot (about 3 large)
¾ cup chopped celery
⅓ cup raisins
⅓ cup coarsely chopped walnuts
¾ cup fat-free mayonnaise
½ teaspoon Dijon-style mustard
1–2 teaspoons sugar
⅛ teaspoon salt
Lettuce leaves, as garnish

1. Combine carrot, celery, raisins, and walnuts in medium bowl. Add remaining ingredients, except lettuce, stirring until blended. Serve on lettuce-lined salad plates.

Nutritional Data

PER SERVING		EXCHANGES	
Calories:	115	Milk:	0.0
% Calories from fat:	30	Vegetable:	2.0
Fat (gm):	4.1	Fruit:	0.5
Sat. fat (gm):	0.3	Bread:	0.0
Cholesterol (mg):	0	Meat:	0.0
Sodium (mg):	460	Fat:	1.0
Protein (gm):	2.6		
Carbohydrate (gm):	19.2		

CREAMY POTATO SALAD

Thanks to fat-free mayonnaise, it's possible to include hard-cooked egg and crisp bacon pieces in this salad. For the creamiest salad, toss the potatoes with the dressing while they're still slightly warm.

10 Servings (about ⅔ cup each)

1½ pounds russet potatoes, peeled, cut into ¾-inch cubes
1 cup sliced celery
½ cup thinly sliced green onions and tops
¼ cup chopped green bell pepper
¼ cup chopped red bell pepper
½ cup chopped sweet pickle, *or* pickle relish
2 hard-cooked eggs, chopped
4 slices bacon, fried, well drained, crumbled
1 cup fat-free mayonnaise
½ cup fat-free sour cream
2 tablespoons cider vinegar
1 tablespoon prepared mustard
½ teaspoon celery seed
Salt and pepper, to taste

1. Cook potatoes, covered, in 2 inches simmering water until fork-tender, about 10 minutes. Drain and cool until just warm.

2. Combine potatoes, celery, green onion, green and red bell pepper, sweet pickle, eggs, and bacon in large bowl. In small bowl, mix remaining ingredients, except salt and pepper; spoon over vegetable mixture and toss. Season to taste with salt and pepper.

Nutritional Data

PER SERVING		EXCHANGES	
Calories:	132	Milk:	0.1
% Calories from fat:	16	Vegetable:	0.2
Fat (gm):	2.5	Fruit:	0.0
Sat. fat (gm):	0.8	Bread:	1.3
Cholesterol (mg):	44.7	Meat:	0.3
Sodium (mg):	495	Fat:	0.3
Protein (gm):	4.3		
Carbohydrate (gm):	24.5		

GERMAN POTATO SALAD

Tart and tangy in flavor, this salad is best served warm from the skillet.

6 Servings (about ²/₃ cup each)

3 slices bacon
1 cup chopped onion
1 tablespoon flour
¹/₂ cup reduced-sodium beef broth
1¹/₄ cups cider vinegar
1 tablespoon sugar
¹/₂ teaspoon celery seed
1¹/₂ pounds potatoes, peeled, sliced, and cooked, warm
Salt and pepper, to taste
2 tablespoons finely chopped parsley leaves

1. Cook bacon in medium skillet until crisp; drain and crumble bacon. Discard all but 1 tablespoon bacon fat; add onion to skillet and saute until tender and browned, about 5 minutes. Stir in flour; cook 1 minute.

2. Add broth, vinegar, sugar, and celery seed to onion mixture and heat to boiling; boil, stirring constantly, until thickened, 1 to 2 minutes. Pour mixture over warm potatoes in bowl and toss. Season to taste with salt and pepper; sprinkle with parsley. Serve warm.

Nutritional Data

PER SERVING		EXCHANGES	
Calories:	133	Milk:	0.0
% Calories from fat:	11	Vegetable:	0.0
Fat (gm):	1.8	Fruit:	0.0
Sat. fat (gm):	0.6	Bread:	2.0
Cholesterol (mg):	2.7	Meat:	0.0
Sodium (mg):	64	Fat:	0.0
Protein (gm):	3.6		
Carbohydrate (gm):	29.5		

MACARONI SALAD

◆

Fourth of July signals fried chicken, apple pie, and, of course, homemade macaroni salad! Add 1 cup halved or quartered summer-ripe cherry tomatoes for festive color.

6 Servings (about ⅔ cup each)

2 cups cooked elbow macaroni
1 cup frozen baby peas, thawed
½ cup chopped onion
½ cup chopped celery
⅓ cup shredded carrot
¼ cup chopped red bell pepper
¼ cup sliced ripe, *or* pimiento-stuffed, olives
¾ cup fat-free mayonnaise
2 teaspoons prepared mustard
1 teaspoon sugar
Salt and pepper, to taste

1. Combine macaroni, peas, onion, celery, carrot, bell pepper, and olives in medium bowl. Add mayonnaise, mustard, and sugar and stir until blended. Season to taste with salt and pepper.

Note

Other pasta, such as rotini, fusilli, ziti, or shells, can be substituted for the macaroni.

Nutritional Data

PER SERVING		EXCHANGES	
Calories:	129	Milk:	0.0
% Calories from fat:	9	Vegetable:	0.0
Fat (gm):	1.3	Fruit:	0.0
Sat. fat (gm):	0.2	Bread:	1.5
Cholesterol (mg):	0	Meat:	0.0
Sodium (mg):	583	Fat:	0.0
Protein (gm):	4		
Carbohydrate (gm):	25.6		

FREEZER COLESLAW

◆

A colorful slaw that is easy to make and convenient to have on hand.

8 Servings (about ³/₄ cup each)

1½ pounds red cabbage, thinly sliced
2 carrots, shredded or thinly sliced
1 red bell pepper, chopped
1 small onion, thinly sliced
  Salt, to taste
1 cup water
³/₄ cup cider vinegar
1²/₃ cups sugar
1 teaspoon caraway seed

1. Layer cabbage, carrots, bell pepper, and onion in colander, sprinkling each layer lightly with salt; let stand 1 hour. Rinse well under cold running water; drain.

2. Heat remaining ingredients to boiling in small saucepan; reduce heat and simmer, uncovered, 5 minutes. Cool to room temperature.

3. Mix vegetables and sugar syrup. Pack coleslaw in freezer containers or bags and freeze. To serve, thaw in refrigerator or at room temperature.

Nutritional Data

PER SERVING		EXCHANGES	
Calories:	205	Milk:	0.0
% Calories from fat:	1	Vegetable:	2.0
Fat (gm):	0.4	Fruit:	0.0
Sat. fat (gm):	0	Bread:	2.0
Cholesterol (mg):	0	Meat:	0.0
Sodium (mg):	20	Fat:	0.0
Protein (gm):	1.9		
Carbohydrate (gm):	53.1		

WALDORF SALAD

◆

Using both red and green apples adds color and flavor interest. If your family enjoys this salad with miniature marshmallows, please add them!

4 Servings (about ³/₄ cup each)

2 cups cored, cubed red and green apples
1 cup sliced celery
¼ cup raisins
¼ cup coarsely chopped, toasted walnuts,
  or pecans
¼ cup fat-free mayonnaise
¼ cup fat-free sour cream
2–3 teaspoons lemon juice
1–2 tablespoons honey
  Lettuce leaves, as garnish

1. Combine apples, celery, raisins, and walnuts in medium bowl. Mix remaining ingredients, except lettuce leaves, and stir into apple mixture. Serve on lettuce-lined plates.

Nutritional Data

PER SERVING		EXCHANGES	
Calories:	149	Milk:	0.0
% Calories from fat:	26	Vegetable:	0.5
Fat (gm):	4.7	Fruit:	1.5
Sat. fat (gm):	0.3	Bread:	0.0
Cholesterol (mg):	0	Meat:	0.0
Sodium (mg):	227	Fat:	1.0
Protein (gm):	3.5		
Carbohydrate (gm):	26.5		

WILTED SPINACH SALAD

---◆---

A delicious favorite that includes the bacon but not the fat!

4 Servings

1 package (10 ounces) salad spinach, rinsed, dried
4 green onions and tops, sliced
4 slices bacon, fried crisp, well drained, crumbled
1 cup fat-free bottled French dressing, *or* sweet-sour salad dressing
1 hard-cooked egg, chopped
Salt and pepper, to taste

1. Combine spinach, onion, and bacon in salad bowl. Heat French dressing to boiling in small saucepan; immediately pour over salad and toss. Sprinkle egg over salad. Season to taste with salt and pepper.

Nutritional Data

PER SERVING		EXCHANGES	
Calories:	95	Milk:	0.0
% Calories from fat:	26	Vegetable:	1.0
Fat (gm):	2.6	Fruit:	0.0
Sat. fat (gm):	0.8	Bread:	0.5
Cholesterol (mg):	38.2	Meat:	0.0
Sodium (mg):	418	Fat:	0.5
Protein (gm):	3.4		
Carbohydrate (gm):	12.6		

CAESAR SALAD

◆

Although anchovies are traditional in this salad we've made them optional because of their high sodium content. If you use anchovies, drain them well as they are packed in oil.

4 Servings

4 thick slices French, *or* Italian, bread
1 clove garlic, cut in half
6 cups torn romaine lettuce
2 tablespoons lemon juice
2 tablespoons real egg product
1 tablespoon olive oil
½ teaspoon Worcestershire sauce
2–3 anchovies, well drained, chopped (optional)
2 tablespoons grated fat-free Parmesan cheese
⅛ teaspoon dry mustard
   Dash red pepper sauce
   Freshly ground pepper, to taste

1. Rub both sides of bread slices with cut side of garlic; mince remaining garlic and reserve. Cut bread into ½ to ¾ inch cubes. Bake on jelly roll pan at 425° until croutons are toasted, about 5 minutes.

2. Place lettuce in salad bowl. Beat together lemon juice, reserved garlic, and remaining ingredients, except croutons and pepper. Pour dressing over lettuce and toss; season to taste with pepper. Add croutons and toss again.

Note

As eating raw egg (traditional in Caesar salad) is not recommended, the recipe includes real egg product, which is pasteurized and safe to eat.

Nutritional Data

PER SERVING		EXCHANGES	
Calories:	127	Milk:	0.0
% Calories from fat:	30	Vegetable:	1.0
Fat (gm):	4.4	Fruit:	0.0
Sat. fat (gm):	0.6	Bread:	1.0
Cholesterol (mg):	0	Meat:	0.0
Sodium (mg):	200	Fat:	0.5
Protein (gm):	5.3		
Carbohydrate (gm):	17.1		

TEN-LAYER SALAD

Or make this salad as many layers as you want! Add a layer of cubed chicken breast or lean smoked ham for an entrée salad, using 3 ounces of cooked meat per person.

6 to 8 Servings

2 cups thinly sliced romaine lettuce
1 cup thinly sliced red cabbage
1 medium red, *or* green, bell pepper, sliced
1 cup broccoli, *or* cauliflower, florets
1 cup sliced mushrooms
1 cup sliced carrot
1 cup halved cherry tomatoes
1/2 cup sliced cucumber
1/2 cup sliced red onion
　Herbed Sour Cream Dressing (recipe follows)
　Finely chopped parsley leaves, as garnish

1. Arrange lettuce in bottom of 1 1/2-quart glass bowl; arrange remaining vegetables in layers over lettuce. Spread dressing over top of salad and sprinkle with parsley. Refrigerate, loosely covered, 8 hours or overnight. Toss before serving.

Herbed Sour Cream Dressing

Makes about 1 1/2 cups

3/4 cup fat-free mayonnaise
3/4 cup fat-free sour cream
2–3 cloves garlic, minced
1/2 teaspoon dried basil
1/2 teaspoon dried tarragon
1/4 teaspoon salt
1/8 teaspoon pepper

1. Mix all ingredients in small bowl; refrigerate until ready to use.

Nutritional Data

PER SERVING		EXCHANGES	
Calories:	91	Milk:	0.0
% Calories from fat:	4	Vegetable:	2.0
Fat (gm):	0.5	Fruit:	0.0
Sat. fat (gm):	0.1	Bread:	0.5
Cholesterol (mg):	0	Meat:	0.0
Sodium (mg):	506	Fat:	0.0
Protein (gm):	4.4		
Carbohydrate (gm):	19.7		

9
SANDWICHES

Sloppy Joes

Cheeseburgers Supreme

Crab Melt

Monte Cristo

SLOPPY JOES

───────◆───────

*A comfort food I remember fondly as a youngster,
taken from my mother's recipe file. Toasted buns
are a must for this sweet-sour filling.*

4 Servings (about 1/2 cup each)

1 pound ground beef eye of round steak, *or* 95%
  lean ground beef
1/2 cup chopped onion
1/2 cup finely chopped celery
1/2 cup finely chopped red, *or* green, bell pepper
2 cloves garlic, minced
1 cup reduced-sodium catsup
1/2 cup water
2 tablespoons prepared mustard
1 tablespoon cider vinegar
2 teaspoons packed light brown sugar
  Salt and pepper, to taste
4 hamburger buns, toasted

1. Cook ground beef, onion, celery, bell pepper, and garlic in medium
skillet over medium heat until beef is browned and vegetables tender,
about 10 minutes.

2. Stir in catsup, water, mustard, vinegar, and brown sugar; heat to boiling. Reduce heat and simmer, uncovered, until mixture is thickened,
about 5 minutes. Season to taste with salt and pepper. Spoon into
toasted buns.

Variation

Baked Sloppy Potatoes: Instead of buns, use 4 large baked potatoes.
Loosen the flesh with a fork; spoon meat filling over.

Nutritional Data

PER SERVING		EXCHANGES	
Calories:	385	Milk:	0.0
% Calories from fat:	17	Vegetable:	2.0
Fat (gm):	7.4	Fruit:	0.0
Sat. fat (gm):	2.2	Bread:	2.0
Cholesterol (mg):	64	Meat:	3.5
Sodium (mg):	423	Fat:	0.0
Protein (gm):	32.5		
Carbohydrate (gm):	48.2		

CHEESEBURGERS SUPREME

---◆---

Top these moist burgers with your choice of catsup, mustard, raw or sauteed onions, sauteed mushrooms, or chopped olives, and serve with plenty of dill pickles and Crispy Fries (see p. 82).

4 Servings

1 pound ground beef eye of round steak, *or* 95% lean ground beef
2–4 tablespoons finely chopped onion
3 tablespoons water
1/2 teaspoon salt
1/4 teaspoon pepper
Vegetable cooking spray
4 slices (1 ounce each) fat-free, *or* reduced-fat, Cheddar, *or* Swiss, cheese
4 hamburger buns, toasted

1. Mix ground beef, onion, water, salt, and pepper in medium bowl just until blended. Shape mixture into four 1-inch thick patties.

2. Spray skillet with cooking spray; heat over medium heat until hot. Cook burgers to desired degree of doneness, 3 to 4 minutes per side for medium. Top each burger with slice of cheese; cover skillet and cook until cheese is beginning to melt, 1 to 2 minutes. Serve burgers in buns.

Nutritional Data

PER SERVING		EXCHANGES	
Calories:	326	Milk:	0.0
% Calories from fat:	19	Vegetable:	0.0
Fat (gm):	6.7	Fruit:	0.0
Sat. fat (gm):	2.2	Bread:	1.5
Cholesterol (mg):	64	Meat:	4.0
Sodium (mg):	768	Fat:	0.0
Protein (gm):	39.5		
Carbohydrate (gm):	24.1		

CRAB MELT

◆

Canned tuna packed in water, boiled shrimp, or surimi (imitation crab meat) can be used in place of the crab.

2 Servings

4 ounces cooked crab meat, flaked
2 tablespoons chopped red bell pepper
1 medium green onion, thinly sliced
2 tablespoons fat-free mayonnaise
2 tablespoons fat-free sour cream
1/4–1/2 teaspoon dried dill weed
1–2 teaspoons lemon juice
Salt and pepper, to taste
2 slices white, *or* wholewheat, bread
2 slices (3/4 ounce each) fat-free American cheese

1. Mix crab, bell pepper, green onion, mayonnaise, sour cream, and dill weed in small bowl; season to taste with lemon juice, salt, and pepper. Spread on bread slices and top with cheese.

2. Bake at 400°, or broil, until sandwiches are warm and cheese melted.

Nutritional Data

PER SERVING		EXCHANGES	
Calories:	182	Milk:	0.0
% Calories from fat:	10	Vegetable:	0.0
Fat (gm):	2	Fruit:	0.0
Sat. fat (gm):	0.3	Bread:	1.0
Cholesterol (mg):	56.7	Meat:	2.0
Sodium (mg):	786	Fat:	0.0
Protein (gm):	19.9		
Carbohydrate (gm):	20.4		

MONTE CRISTO

The sourdough bread and egg batter coating make this grilled sandwich special. Substitute any desired meat and cheese for variation.

4 Servings

- 4 slices lean smoked ham (3 ounces)
- 4 slices turkey, *or* chicken, breast (3 ounces)
- 4 slices fat-free Cheddar cheese (4 ounces)
- 8 slices sourdough, *or* Italian, bread
- ¹/₂ cup real egg product, *or* 4 egg whites, beaten
- Vegetable cooking spray

1. Arrange meats and cheese on 4 slices of bread; top with remaining bread. Pour egg product into pie pan; dip sandwiches in egg, coating both sides.

2. Spray large skillet with cooking spray; heat over medium heat until hot. Cook sandwiches over medium to medium-low heat until browned, about 5 minutes on each side.

Nutritional Data

PER SERVING		EXCHANGES	
Calories:	248	Milk:	0.0
% Calories from fat:	9	Vegetable:	0.0
Fat (gm):	2.4	Fruit:	0.0
Sat. fat (gm):	0.5	Bread:	2.0
Cholesterol (mg):	27.7	Meat:	2.0
Sodium (mg):	756	Fat:	0.0
Protein (gm):	26.8		
Carbohydrate (gm):	28.9		

10
BREADS

Garlic Bread

Vinegar Biscuits

Bubble Loaf

English Muffin Bread

French Toast

Banana Bread

Sticky Buns

GARLIC BREAD

*Select a good quality French or Italian loaf for this aromatic bread,
or use a sourdough bread for an interesting flavor variation.*

4 Servings
4 thick slices French, *or* Italian, bread
   Olive oil cooking spray
2 cloves garlic, cut into halves

1. Spray both sides of bread generously with cooking spray. Broil on cookie sheet 4 inches from heat source until browned, about 1 minute on each side.

2. Rub both sides of hot toast with cut sides of garlic.

Variation

Parmesan Garlic Bread: Combine 2 teaspoons grated Parmesan cheese and 1 teaspoon minced garlic. Spray bread with cooking spray as above, and spread top of each slice with cheese mixture. Broil as above, or wrap loosely in aluminum foil and bake at 350° until warm, about 5 minutes.

Nutritional Data

PER SERVING		EXCHANGES	
Calories:	71	Milk:	0.0
% Calories from fat:	10	Vegetable:	0.0
Fat (gm):	0.8	Fruit:	0.0
Sat. fat (gm):	0.2	Bread:	1.0
Cholesterol (mg):	0	Meat:	0.0
Sodium (mg):	152	Fat:	0.0
Protein (gm):	2.3		
Carbohydrate (gm):	13.5		

VINEGAR BISCUITS

---◆---

Every grandmother no doubt had her
version of this old-fashioned biscuit recipe.

12 Biscuits (1 per serving)

- ³⁄₄ cup skim milk
- ¹⁄₄ cup cider vinegar
- 2 cups all-purpose flour
- 1¹⁄₂ teaspoons baking soda
- 1 teaspoon cream of tartar
- ¹⁄₂ teaspoon salt
- 3 tablespoons vegetable shortening, melted

1. Mix milk and vinegar in glass measure. Combine flour, baking soda, cream of tartar, and salt in medium bowl; add milk mixture and shortening, mixing until blended.

2. Knead dough on generously floured surface 1 to 2 minutes. Pat dough into ¹⁄₂ inch thickness; cut into biscuits with 3-inch-round cutter. Bake on greased cookie sheet at 425° until golden, 10 to 12 minutes.

Nutritional Data

PER SERVING		EXCHANGES	
Calories:	109	Milk:	0.0
% Calories from fat:	27	Vegetable:	0.0
Fat (gm):	3.2	Fruit:	0.0
Sat. fat (gm):	0.8	Bread:	1.0
Cholesterol (mg):	0.3	Meat:	0.0
Sodium (mg):	255	Fat:	0.5
Protein (gm):	2.7		
Carbohydrate (gm):	17.1		

BUBBLE LOAF

*Also called Bath Buns and Monkey Bread, this pull-apart
loaf is easy to make, fun to eat, and perfect for
potluck offerings and parties. The recipe can be halved
and baked in a 6-cup fluted cake pan.*

16 Servings

2 packages active dry yeast
1 cup skim milk, warm (110°)
6 tablespoons margarine, softened
¼ cup sugar
3 eggs
4 cups all-purpose flour
½ teaspoon salt

1. Stir yeast into milk; let stand 2 to 3 minutes. In a large bowl, beat margarine and sugar until fluffy; beat in eggs, 1 at a time. Mix in combined flour and salt alternately with milk mixture, beginning and ending with dry ingredients and beating well after each addition. Let stand, covered, in warm place until dough is double in size, about 1 hour. Punch dough down.

2. Drop dough by large spoonfuls into greased 10-inch tube pan. Let rise, covered, until dough is double in size, about 30 minutes. Bake at 350° until browned, 25 to 30 minutes. Cool in pan on wire rack 10 minutes; remove from pan. Serve warm.

Nutritional Data

PER SERVING		EXCHANGES	
Calories:	186	Milk:	0.0
% Calories from fat:	27	Vegetable:	0.0
Fat (gm):	5.5	Fruit:	0.0
Sat. fat (gm):	1.2	Bread:	2.0
Cholesterol (mg):	40.2	Meat:	0.0
Sodium (mg):	137	Fat:	1.0
Protein (gm):	5.3		
Carbohydrate (gm):	28.3		

ENGLISH MUFFIN BREAD

◆

*This quick and easy single-rise bread has a coarse texture similar
to English muffins. Delicious warm from the oven, or toasted.*

16 Servings

Vegetable cooking spray
1–2 teaspoons yellow cornmeal
2–2½ cups all-purpose flour, divided
½ cup quick-cooking oats
1 package active dry yeast
1 teaspoon salt
1¼ cups skim milk
1 tablespoon honey
¼ teaspoon baking soda

1. Spray 8 x 4 x 2-inch loaf pan with cooking spray; coat with cornmeal.

2. Combine 1½ cups flour, oats, yeast, and salt in large bowl. Heat milk
   and honey until warm (110-120°) in small saucepan; stir in baking
   soda. Add milk mixture to flour mixture, mixing until smooth. Stir in
   enough of remaining ½ cup flour to make a thick batter. Pour into prepared pan. Let rise, covered, in warm place until doubled in size, 45 to
   60 minutes.

3. Bake at 400° until bread is golden and sounds hollow when tapped, 25
   to 30 minutes. Remove from pan immediately and cool on wire rack.

Variation

Raisin Bread: Spray loaf pan, but do not coat with cornmeal. Stir 1 teaspoon cinnamon and ½ cup raisins into batter.

Nutritional Data

PER SERVING		EXCHANGES	
Calories:	79	Milk:	0.0
% Calories from fat:	4	Vegetable:	0.0
Fat (gm):	0.4	Fruit:	0.0
Sat. fat (gm):	0.1	Bread:	1.0
Cholesterol (mg):	0.3	Meat:	0.0
Sodium (mg):	163	Fat:	0.0
Protein (gm):	2.9		
Carbohydrate (gm):	15.9		

FRENCH TOAST

◆

A rich breakfast entrée with a sweet surprise inside!
Serve with warm maple syrup or a drizzle of honey.

4 Servings

3 eggs, *or* ³/₄ cup real egg product
¹/₃ cup fat-free half-and-half, *or* skim milk
1 teaspoon ground cinnamon
¹/₄ teaspoon ground nutmeg
4 thick (1 inch) slices sourdough, *or* Italian,
   bread
4 tablespoons fat-free cream cheese
4 teaspoons strawberry, *or* other flavor,
   spreadable fruit preserves
1–2 tablespoons margarine
1 cup maple syrup, *or* pancake syrup, warm

1. Combine eggs, half-and-half, and spices in shallow bowl.

2. Cut a pocket in the side of each bread slice; fill with cream cheese and spreadable fruit. Soak bread in egg mixture, turning to soak both sides.

3. Cook bread in margarine in large skillet on low to medium-low heat until browned, about 5 minutes on each side. Serve with warm syrup.

Nutritional Data

PER SERVING		EXCHANGES	
Calories:	390	Milk:	0.0
% Calories from fat:	17	Vegetable:	0.0
Fat (gm):	7.5	Fruit:	3.5
Sat. fat (gm):	1.9	Bread:	1.0
Cholesterol (mg):	159.8	Meat:	1.0
Sodium (mg):	346	Fat:	1.0
Protein (gm):	9.7		
Carbohydrate (gm):	70.9		

BANANA BREAD

*Brown sugar gives this banana bread a caramel flavor,
the applesauce adds moistness. It's the best!*

16 Servings

4 tablespoons margarine, softened
1/4 cup applesauce
2 eggs
2 tablespoons skim milk, *or* water
3/4 cup packed light brown sugar
1 cup mashed banana (2 to 3 medium bananas)
1 3/4 cups all-purpose flour
2 teaspoons baking powder
1/2 teaspoon baking soda
1/4 teaspoon salt
1/4 cup coarsely chopped walnuts, *or* pecans

1. Beat margarine, applesauce, eggs, milk, and brown sugar in large mixing bowl until smooth. Add banana and blend at low speed; beat at high speed 1 to 2 minutes.

2. Combine flour, baking powder, baking soda, and salt; mix into batter. Mix in walnuts. Pour batter into greased loaf pan, 8 x 4 x 2 inches.

3. Bake at 350° until bread is golden and toothpick inserted in center comes out clean, 55 to 60 minutes. Cool in pan on wire rack 10 minutes; remove from pan and cool to room temperature.

Nutritional Data

PER SERVING		EXCHANGES	
Calories:	151	Milk:	0.0
% Calories from fat:	28	Vegetable:	0.0
Fat (gm):	4.8	Fruit:	0.5
Sat. fat (gm):	0.9	Bread:	1.0
Cholesterol (mg):	26.7	Meat:	0.0
Sodium (mg):	160	Fat:	1.0
Protein (gm):	2.9		
Carbohydrate (gm):	24.9		

STICKY BUNS

Impossible to resist, especially when the buns are fresh from the oven! Finger licking is permitted!

24 Buns (1 per serving)

3½ cups all-purpose flour, divided
⅓ cup plus 2 tablespoons sugar, divided
1 package active dry yeast
1 tablespoon plus 1 teaspoon ground cinnamon, divided
1 teaspoon salt
1 cup warm skim milk (115°)
¼ cup fat-free sour cream
1 egg, beaten
 Grated rind from 1 orange
 Vegetable cooking spray
 Sticky Bun Topping (recipe follows)
½ cup pecan pieces

1. Combine 2 cups flour, ⅓ cup sugar, yeast, 1 tablespoon cinnamon, and salt in large bowl. Stir in milk, sour cream, egg, and orange rind until smooth. Stir in enough remaining 1½ cups flour to make soft dough. Knead dough on floured surface until smooth and elastic, about 5 minutes. Place in greased bowl; turn greased side up, and let stand, covered, in warm place until doubled in size, 30 to 45 minutes. Punch dough down.

2. Spray three 9-inch-round cake pans with cooking spray; spoon about ½ cup hot Sticky Bun Topping into each and sprinkle with pecan pieces.

3. Combine remaining 2 tablespoons sugar and 1 teaspoon cinnamon in small bowl. Divide dough in half. Roll half the dough on floured surface into rectangle 12 x 7 inches; sprinkle with half the sugar mixture. Roll dough up, beginning with long side; cut into 12 equal slices. Repeat with remaining dough and sugar mixture. Place 8 rolls, cut sides up, in each pan, over the topping.

4. Let rolls rise, covered in warm place, until doubled in size, about 30 minutes. Bake at 375° until golden, 15 to 20 minutes. Immediately invert rolls onto aluminum foil.

Sticky Bun Topping

4 tablespoons margarine
1½ cups packed light brown sugar
½ cup light corn syrup
¼ cup all-purpose flour

1. Melt margarine in small saucepan; stir in remaining ingredients, and cook until bubbly.

Variation

Cinnamon Rolls: Do not make Sticky Bun Topping. Make dough as above, mixing in ½ cup raisins. Let dough rise, then roll and shape as above, sprinkling with double the amount of sugar and cinnamon. Place rolls, cut sides up, in sprayed muffin cups. Bake as above, and invert rolls onto wire racks. Mix 2 cups powdered sugar with enough milk to make a thick glaze; drizzle over slightly warm rolls.

Nutritional Data

PER SERVING		EXCHANGES	
Calories:	200	Milk:	0.0
% Calories from fat:	17	Vegetable:	0.0
Fat (gm):	3.8	Fruit:	0.0
Sat. fat (gm):	0.6	Bread:	2.5
Cholesterol (mg):	9	Meat:	0.0
Sodium (mg):	131	Fat:	0.5
Protein (gm):	3.1		
Carbohydrate (gm):	38.9		

11
CAKES

Sour Cream Coffee Cake with Apple-Date Filling

Glazed Orange Chiffon Cake

Lemon Pound Cake

Chocolate Buttermilk Cake with Mocha Frosting

Carrot Cake with Cream Cheese Frosting

Spice Cake with Penuche Frosting

Pineapple Upside-Down Cake

Boston Cream Pie

Ice Cream Jelly Roll Cake

Sour Cream Coffee Cake with Apple-Date Filling

An irresistible offering, this moist cake is filled with apples, dates, sugar, and spices. Serve warm, if desired.

16 Servings

$^1\!/_2$ cup margarine, softened
$^1\!/_4$ cup unsweetened applesauce
1 cup granulated sugar
$^1\!/_2$ cup packed light brown sugar
3 eggs
$1^1\!/_2$ teaspoons vanilla
3 cups all-purpose flour
$1^1\!/_2$ teaspoons baking powder
$1^1\!/_2$ teaspoons baking soda
1 teaspoon ground cinnamon
$^1\!/_2$ teaspoon salt
$1^1\!/_2$ cups fat-free sour cream
Apple-Date Filling (recipe follows)
Cream Cheese Glaze (recipe follows)

1. Beat margarine, applesauce, and sugars until smooth. Beat in eggs, 1 at a time; beat in vanilla. Combine flour, baking powder, baking soda, cinnamon, and salt and mix in alternately with sour cream, beginning and ending with dry ingredients.

2. Spoon $^1\!/_3$ of batter into greased and floured 12-cup fluted cake pan; spoon $^1\!/_2$ of Apple-Date Filling over batter. Repeat layers, ending with batter.

3. Bake at 325° until toothpick inserted in center of cake comes out clean, about 1 hour. Cool in pan on wire rack 10 minutes; remove from pan and cool to room temperature.

4. Place coffee cake on serving plate; spoon glaze over.

Apple-Date Filling

Makes about 1 cup

$^1\!/_2$ cup dried apples, coarsely chopped
$^1\!/_4$ cup chopped dates
$^2\!/_3$ cup water

⅓ cup packed light brown sugar
1 tablespoon flour
¼ teaspoon ground nutmeg
⅛ teaspoon salt

1. Combine all ingredients in small saucepan and heat to boiling; reduce heat and simmer, uncovered, until apples are tender and mixture is thick, 5 to 8 minutes. Cool.

Cream Cheese Glaze

Makes ½ cup

2 ounces fat-free cream cheese, room temperature
1 cup powdered sugar

1. Beat cream cheese and powdered sugar until smooth; refrigerate until ready to use.

Nutritional Data

PER SERVING		EXCHANGES	
Calories:	306	Milk:	0.0
% Calories from fat:	20	Vegetable:	0.0
Fat (gm):	6.9	Fruit:	1.0
Sat. fat (gm):	1.4	Bread:	2.5
Cholesterol (mg):	39.9	Meat:	0.0
Sodium (mg):	353	Fat:	1.5
Protein (gm):	5.7		
Carbohydrate (gm):	56.4		

GLAZED ORANGE CHIFFON CAKE

Sometimes called Sunshine Cake, this cake has a perfect, tender texture and a delicate orange flavor.

12 Servings

2¼ cups cake flour (not sifted)
1⅔ cups granulated sugar
1 tablespoon baking powder
¼ teaspoon salt
¾ cup orange juice, *or* water
⅓ cup vegetable oil
5 egg yolks
1 teaspoon vanilla
2 teaspoons grated orange rind
7 egg whites
½ teaspoon cream of tartar
2 cups powdered sugar
2–3 tablespoons orange juice
Ground nutmeg, as garnish

1. Combine flour, granulated sugar, baking powder, and salt in large mixing bowl. Mix orange juice, oil, egg yolks, vanilla, and orange rind in bowl; add to flour mixture and beat at medium speed until smooth.

2. With clean beaters and in separate large bowl, beat egg whites until foamy. Add cream of tartar and beat to very stiff but not dry peaks. Stir about ¼ of egg whites into cake batter; fold batter into remaining egg whites. Pour batter into ungreased 10-inch tube pan.

3. Bake at 325° until cake is golden and springs back when touched (cracks in top of cake will appear dry), 55 to 60 minutes. Invert cake pan on a funnel or bottle until cake is completely cool. Loosen side of cake and invert onto serving plate.

4. Mix powdered sugar with enough orange juice to make glaze consistency. Spoon glaze over top of cool cake; sprinkle with nutmeg.

Nutritional Data

PER SERVING		EXCHANGES	
Calories:	358	Milk:	0.0
% Calories from fat:	21	Vegetable:	0.0
Fat (gm):	8.4	Fruit:	0.0
Sat. fat (gm):	1.5	Bread:	4.0
Cholesterol (mg):	88.8	Meat:	0.0
Sodium (mg):	163	Fat:	1.5
Protein (gm):	5		
Carbohydrate (gm):	66.3		

LEMON POUND CAKE

*Made in a fluted cake pan, this luscious cake is
perfect for special occasions.*

12 Servings

³/₄ cup sugar
¹/₃ cup margarine, softened
1 cup reduced-fat sour cream
3 egg whites
2 teaspoons lemon juice
1 tablespoon lemon rind, grated
2¹/₂ cups cake flour (not sifted)
1 teaspoon baking soda
¹/₄ teaspoon salt
Lemon Syrup (recipe follows)
Powdered sugar, as garnish

1. Beat sugar, margarine, and sour cream in large bowl until smooth; beat in egg whites, lemon juice, and rind. Mix in combined flour, baking soda, and salt; beat until smooth, about 1 minute. Spoon batter into greased and floured 6-cup fluted cake pan.

2. Bake at 350° until toothpick inserted in center of cake comes out clean, 40 to 50 minutes. Cool in pan on wire rack 20 minutes; invert onto cooling rack.

3. Pierce cake at 1-inch intervals with long-tined fork or skewer; spoon warm syrup over cake. Sprinkle generously with powdered sugar before serving.

Lemon Syrup

Makes about ³/₄ cup

2/3 cup powdered sugar
1/4 cup lemon juice
3 tablespoons water

1. Combine sugar, lemon juice, and water in small saucepan; heat to boiling, stirring until sugar is dissolved. Cool slightly before using.

Variation

Lemon Poppy Seed Pound Cake: Mix 2 tablespoons poppy seed into cake batter. Instead of Lemon Syrup, mix 1¹/₂ cups powdered sugar with enough lemon juice to make glaze consistency. Spoon glaze over cake; sprinkle lightly with poppy seed. Garnish with lemon rind twists.

Nutritional Data

PER SERVING		EXCHANGES	
Calories:	247	Milk:	0.0
% Calories from fat:	24	Vegetable:	0.0
Fat (gm):	6.5	Fruit:	0.0
Sat. fat (gm):	1	Bread:	3.0
Cholesterol (mg):	6.3	Meat:	0.0
Sodium (mg):	235	Fat:	1.0
Protein (gm):	3.5		
Carbohydrate (gm):	43.3		

CHOCOLATE BUTTERMILK CAKE WITH MOCHA FROSTING

A chocolate dream come true, this cake is 3 layers high and generously covered with creamy mocha frosting!

16 Servings

6 tablespoons vegetable shortening
1 cup granulated sugar
1/2 cup packed light brown sugar
2 eggs
2 egg whites
1 teaspoon vanilla
2 cups cake flour
1/2 cup unsweetened cocoa
2 teaspoons baking powder
1/2 teaspoon baking soda
1/2 teaspoon salt
1 cup buttermilk
Mocha Frosting (recipe follow)

1. Grease and flour three 8-inch-round cake pans. Line bottoms of pans with waxed paper.

2. Beat shortening, sugars, eggs, egg whites, and vanilla in large bowl until smooth. Mix in combined flour, cocoa, baking powder, baking soda, and salt alternately with buttermilk, beginning and ending with dry ingredients.

3. Pour batter into prepared pans. Bake at 350° until toothpicks inserted in centers of cakes come out clean, 25 to 30 minutes. Cool in pans on wire racks 10 minutes; invert onto wire racks. Peel off waxed paper and cool cake layers completely.

4. Place 1 cake layer on serving plate; frost with about 1/2 cup frosting. Repeat with second cake layer and frosting. Top with third cake layer; frost top and side of cake.

Mocha Frosting

Makes about 2¹/₂ cups

  5 cups powdered sugar
¹/₂ cup unsweetened cocoa
2–3 teaspoons instant coffee crystals
1–2 tablespoons margarine, softened
  1 teaspoon vanilla
4–5 tablespoons skim milk

1. Combine powdered sugar, cocoa, coffee crystals, and margarine in large bowl; beat in vanilla and enough milk to make glaze consistency.

Nutritional Data

PER SERVING		EXCHANGES	
Calories:	351	Milk:	0.0
% Calories from fat:	17	Vegetable:	0.0
Fat (gm):	6.9	Fruit:	0.0
Sat. fat (gm):	1.8	Bread:	4.5
Cholesterol (mg):	27.3	Meat:	0.0
Sodium (mg):	195	Fat:	1.0
Protein (gm):	4.1		
Carbohydrate (gm):	71.5		

CARROT CAKE WITH CREAM CHEESE FROSTING

Moist and sweetly spiced, you'll make this cake over and over again.

16 Servings

3 cups shredded carrot
1/2 cup raisins for baking
1 cup packed light brown sugar
1/3 cup vegetable oil
3 eggs
2 cups all-purpose flour
1 teaspoon baking powder
1 teaspoon baking soda
1 teaspoon ground cinnamon
1/4 teaspoon ground allspice
1/4 teaspoon ground nutmeg
1/4 teaspoon salt
Cream Cheese Frosting (recipe follows)

1. Mix carrot, raisins, brown sugar, oil, and eggs in large bowl. Mix in combined remaining ingredients, except Cream Cheese Frosting.

2. Pour batter into 2 greased and floured 8-inch-round cake pans. Bake at 350° until toothpicks inserted in cakes come out clean, 25 to 30 minutes. Cool in pans on wire rack 10 minutes; remove from pans and cool.

3. Place 1 cake layer on serving plate and frost. Top with remaining cake layer; frost top and side of cake.

Cream Cheese Frosting

Makes about 3 cups

1 package (8 ounces) reduced-fat cream cheese, softened
2 tablespoons margarine, softened
4–5 cups powdered sugar
1 teaspoon vanilla

1. Beat cream cheese and margarine in medium bowl until smooth; beat in powdered sugar and vanilla.

Nutritional Data

PER SERVING		EXCHANGES	
Calories:	346	Milk:	0.0
% Calories from fat:	24	Vegetable:	1.0
Fat (gm):	9.7	Fruit:	0.0
Sat. fat (gm):	2.7	Bread:	5.0
Cholesterol (mg):	44.9	Meat:	0.0
Sodium (mg):	255	Fat:	2.0
Protein (gm):	4.7		
Carbohydrate (gm):	62.2		

SPICE CAKE WITH PENUCHE FROSTING

The flavor combination of sweet cake spices and creamy caramel fudge (penuche) frosting is too good to be true!

10 Servings

- 4 tablespoons margarine, softened
- 3/4 cup sugar
- 1 egg
- 1/2 teaspoon vanilla
- 1 1/3 cups all-purpose flour
- 2 teaspoons baking powder
- 3/4 teaspoon ground cinnamon
- 1/4 teaspoon ground nutmeg
- 1/4 teaspoon ground ginger
- 1/4 teaspoon salt
- 2/3 cup skim milk
  Penuche Frosting (recipe follows)

1. Beat margarine, sugar, egg, and vanilla in large bowl until smooth. Mix in combined flour, baking powder, spices, and salt alternately with milk, beginning and ending with dry ingredients. Pour batter into 1 greased and floured 8- or 9-inch-round cake pan.

2. Bake at 350° until cake is browned and springs back when touched, about 40 minutes. Cool in pan on wire rack 10 minutes; remove from pan and cool to room temperature.

3. Place cake on serving plate; spread top and side with Penuche Frosting.

Penuche Frosting

Makes about 2¹/₂ cups

3 tablespoons margarine
¹/₂ cup packed light brown sugar
2–2¹/₂ cups powdered sugar
¹/₂ teaspoon vanilla
2–4 tablespoons skim milk

1. Melt margarine in medium saucepan; stir in brown sugar and cook over medium heat until bubbly. Stir in powdered sugar, vanilla, and enough milk to make spreading consistency.

Note

Use the frosting immediately as it tends to thicken quickly. If frosting becomes too thick, thin with a few drops of hot water.

Nutritional Data

PER SERVING		EXCHANGES	
Calories:	342	Milk:	0.0
% Calories from fat:	23	Vegetable:	0.0
Fat (gm):	8.7	Fruit:	0.0
Sat. fat (gm):	1.8	Bread:	4.0
Cholesterol (mg):	21.6	Meat:	0.0
Sodium (mg):	233	Fat:	1.5
Protein (gm):	3.1		
Carbohydrate (gm):	63.6		

PINEAPPLE UPSIDE-DOWN CAKE

Invert the cake immediately after baking so all the warm caramel topping releases from the pan.

8 to 10 Servings

- 3 tablespoons light corn syrup
- 5 tablespoons margarine, softened, divided
- ²/₃ cup packed light brown sugar
- 2–3 tablespoons chopped pecans
- 1 can (8 ounces) sliced pineapple in its own juice, drained, slices cut in halves
- 4 maraschino cherries, cut in halves
- ²/₃ cup granulated sugar
- 1 egg
- ¹/₂ teaspoon pineapple extract, *or* vanilla
- 1¹/₃ cups all-purpose flour
- 2 teaspoons baking powder
- ¹/₄ teaspoon salt
- ²/₃ cup skim milk
- Light whipped topping, as garnish

1. Heat corn syrup and 1 tablespoon margarine until melted in small skillet. Stir in brown sugar and pecans and cook over medium heat until mixture is bubbly, 2 to 3 minutes. Pour topping mixture into ungreased 9-inch-round cake pan; arrange pineapple slices and cherries on top.

2. Beat remaining 4 tablespoons margarine, granulated sugar, egg, and pineapple extract in medium bowl until smooth. Mix in combined flour, baking powder, and salt alternately with milk, beginning and ending with dry ingredients. Pour batter over topping in pan.

3. Bake at 350° until cake springs back when touched, about 40 minutes. Loosen side of cake with sharp knife and immediately invert onto serving plate. Serve warm with whipped topping.

Nutritional Data

PER SERVING		EXCHANGES	
Calories:	347	Milk:	0.0
% Calories from fat:	23	Vegetable:	0.0
Fat (gm):	9.1	Fruit:	0.5
Sat. fat (gm):	1.7	Bread:	3.5
Cholesterol (mg):	27	Meat:	0.0
Sodium (mg):	264	Fat:	1.5
Protein (gm):	4		
Carbohydrate (gm):	63.8		

BOSTON CREAM PIE

*Called a pie but really a cake, with
chocolatey glaze and a luxurious cream filling.*

12 Servings

    8 tablespoons margarine, softened
1¼ cups sugar
    2 eggs
    1 teaspoon vanilla
2⅔ cups all-purpose flour
    3 teaspoons baking powder
½ teaspoon salt
1⅔ cups skim milk
       Vanilla Cream Filling (recipe follows)
       Chocolate Glaze (recipe follows)

1. Beat margarine, sugar, eggs, and vanilla in medium bowl until smooth. Mix in combined flour, baking powder, and salt alternately with milk, beginning and ending with dry ingredients. Pour batter into 2 greased and floured 8- or 9-inch-round cake pans.

2. Bake at 350° until cakes spring back when touched, about 40 minutes. Cool in pans on wire rack 10 minutes; remove from pans and cool to room temperature.

3. Place 1 cake layer on serving plate; spread with Vanilla Cream Filling. Top with second cake layer and spoon Chocolate Glaze over.

Vanilla Cream Filling

Makes about 1¹/₄ cups

¹/₄ cup sugar
2 tablespoons cornstarch
1 cup skim milk
1 egg, beaten
¹/₂ teaspoon vanilla

1. Mix sugar and cornstarch in saucepan; stir in milk. Heat over medium-high heat, stirring constantly, until mixture comes to a boil; boil, stirring constantly, until thickened.

2. Whisk about ¹/₂ of milk mixture into beaten egg in small bowl; whisk egg mixture back into saucepan. Cook over very low heat, whisking constantly, 30 to 60 seconds. Remove from heat; stir in vanilla and cool.

Chocolate Glaze

1 cup powdered sugar
2 tablespoons unsweetened cocoa
¹/₂ teaspoon vanilla
1–2 tablespoons skim milk

1. Combine powdered sugar and cocoa in small bowl; stir in vanilla and enough milk to make glaze consistency.

Nutritional Data

PER SERVING		EXCHANGES	
Calories:	353	Milk:	0.0
% Calories from fat:	23	Vegetable:	0.0
Fat (gm):	9.3	Fruit:	0.0
Sat. fat (gm):	2	Bread:	4.0
Cholesterol (mg):	54.2	Meat:	0.0
Sodium (mg):	305	Fat:	1.5
Protein (gm):	6.6		
Carbohydrate (gm):	61.3		

ICE CREAM JELLY ROLL CAKE

A versatile cake that can be filled with your flavor choice of fat-free ice cream or frozen yogurt, light whipped topping and sliced fruit, or perhaps Mocha Frosting (see p. 122).

8 Servings

- 3 egg yolks
- 1/2 teaspoon vanilla
- 3/4 cup sugar, divided
- 3 egg whites
- 3/4 cup cake flour (not sifted)
- 1 teaspoon baking powder
- 1/4 teaspoon salt
- 1-1 1/2 quarts strawberry, *or* other flavor, fat-free ice cream, slightly softened
  Powdered sugar, as garnish
  Whole strawberries, as garnish

1. Grease jelly roll pan, 15 1/2 x 10 1/2 x 1 inches. Line bottom of pan with parchment or baking paper; grease and flour paper.

2. Beat egg yolks and vanilla in medium bowl until thick and lemon colored, 3 to 5 minutes. Gradually beat in 1/4 cup sugar, beating 2 minutes longer.

3. Using clean beaters and large bowl, beat egg whites to soft peaks; gradually beat in remaining 1/2 cup granulated sugar, beating to stiff, glossy peaks. Fold egg yolks into whites; sprinkle combined flour, baking powder, and salt over mixture and fold in. Spread batter evenly in prepared pan, using metal spatula.

4. Bake at 375° until cake is golden and springs back when touched, 10 to 12 minutes. Immediately invert cake onto large kitchen towel sprinkled with powdered sugar; peel off paper and discard. Roll cake up in towel, beginning at short end. Cool on wire rack 30 to 60 minutes.

5. Unroll cake; spread with ice cream. Reroll cake and freeze until ice cream is firm, 6 to 8 hours.

6. Trim ends from cake and place cake on serving plate. Sprinkle cake generously with powdered sugar and garnish with strawberries.

Variations

Chocolate Ice Cream Jelly Roll Cake: Make cake as above, adding ¼ cup unsweetened cocoa to the flour mixture. Fill cake with chocolate chip or chocolate fudge fat-free ice cream.

Easy Cake Mix Jelly Roll Cake: Prepare 2 jelly roll pans as above. Replace steps 2 and 3 as follows: Beat 4 eggs in large bowl until thick and lemon colored; mix in ½ cup water. Mix in 1 package (18.25 ounces) yellow or chocolate light cake mix. Spread batter in pans and bake at 325° until cake springs back when touched, 8 to 10 minutes. Complete as above. Makes 2 cakes.

Nutritional Data

PER SERVING		EXCHANGES	
Calories:	229	Milk:	0.0
% Calories from fat:	8	Vegetable:	0.0
Fat (gm):	2	Fruit:	0.0
Sat. fat (gm):	0.6	Bread:	2.5
Cholesterol (mg):	79.9	Meat:	0.0
Sodium (mg):	197	Fat:	0.0
Protein (gm):	7.2		
Carbohydrate (gm):	47.2		

12
COOKIES

Chocolate Chip Cookies

Raisin Oatmeal Cookies

Frosted Sugar Cookies

Tart Lemon Squares

Frosted Cocoa Brownies

CHOCOLATE CHIP COOKIES

◆

Chocolate chip cookies are no doubt
America's favorite—you'll love these.

5 Dozen Cookies

8 tablespoons margarine, softened
1 cup packed light brown sugar
½ cup granulated sugar
1 egg
1 teaspoon vanilla
2½ cups all-purpose flour
1½ teaspoons baking soda
½ teaspoon salt
⅓ cup skim milk
½ package (12-ounce size) reduced-fat semisweet
   chocolate morsels

1. Beat margarine and sugars in medium bowl until fluffy; beat in egg and vanilla. Mix in combined flour, baking soda, and salt alternately with milk, beginning and ending with dry ingredients. Mix in chocolate morsels.

2. Drop cookies by tablespoonfuls onto greased cookie sheets. Bake until browned, about 10 minutes. Cool on wire racks.

Nutritional Data

PER COOKIE		EXCHANGES	
Calories:	66	Milk:	0.0
% Calories from fat:	27	Vegetable:	0.0
Fat (gm):	2	Fruit:	0.0
Sat. fat (gm):	0.7	Bread:	0.5
Cholesterol (mg):	3.6	Meat:	0.0
Sodium (mg):	70	Fat:	0.5
Protein (gm):	0.8		
Carbohydrate (gm):	11.2		

RAISIN OATMEAL COOKIES

Moist and chewy, just the way they should be!

2¹/₂ Dozen Cookies

6 tablespoons margarine, softened
¹/₄ cup fat-free sour cream
1 egg
1 teaspoon vanilla
1 cup packed light brown sugar
1¹/₂ cups quick-cooking oats
1 cup all-purpose flour
¹/₂ teaspoon baking soda
¹/₄ teaspoon baking powder
1 teaspoon ground cinnamon
¹/₂ cup raisins for baking

1. Mix margarine, sour cream, egg, and vanilla in large bowl; beat in brown sugar. Mix in combined oats, flour, baking soda, baking powder, and cinnamon. Mix in raisins.

2. Drop dough onto greased cookie sheets, using 2 tablespoons for each cookie. Bake at 350° until browned, 12 to 15 minutes. Cool on wire racks.

Nutritional Data

PER COOKIE		EXCHANGES	
Calories:	90	Milk:	0.0
% Calories from fat:	27	Vegetable:	0.0
Fat (gm):	2.7	Fruit:	0.0
Sat. fat (gm):	0.5	Bread:	1.0
Cholesterol (mg):	7.1	Meat:	0.0
Sodium (mg):	57	Fat:	0.5
Protein (gm):	1.5		
Carbohydrate (gm):	15.3		

FROSTED SUGAR COOKIES

Rich, crisp, and generously frosted, these cookies will flatter any holiday or special occasion.

6 Dozen Cookies

- 10 tablespoons margarine, softened
- 2 tablespoons fat-free sour cream
- 1 egg
- 1 teaspoon lemon extract
- 1 cup powdered sugar
- 2 cups all-purpose flour
- 1 teaspoon baking powder
- 1/4 teaspoon salt
  Sugar Frosting (recipe follows)
  Ground cinnamon, as garnish

1. Beat margarine, sour cream, egg, and lemon extract in medium bowl until smooth; mix in sugar. Mix in combined flour, baking powder, and salt. Refrigerate dough 4 to 6 hours.

2. Roll dough on floured surface to 1/4 inch thickness. Cut out cookies with 2-inch cookie cutters. Bake at 375° on greased cookie sheets until lightly browned, 8 to 10 minutes. Cool on wire racks.

3. Frost cookies with Sugar Frosting; sprinkle very lightly with cinnamon.

Sugar Frosting

Makes about 3/4 cup

- 2 cups powdered sugar
- 1/2 teaspoon lemon extract, *or* vanilla
- 2–3 tablespoons skim milk

1. In small bowl, mix powdered sugar, lemon extract, and enough milk to make spreadable consistency.

Nutritional Data

PER COOKIE		EXCHANGES	
Calories:	48	Milk:	0.0
% Calories from fat:	31	Vegetable:	0.0
Fat (gm):	1.7	Fruit:	0.0
Sat. fat (gm):	0.3	Bread:	0.5
Cholesterol (mg):	3	Meat:	0.0
Sodium (mg):	45	Fat:	0.5
Protein (gm):	0.5		
Carbohydrate (gm):	7.7		

TART LEMON SQUARES

Another favorite, made skinny!

25 Cookies

3/4 cup all-purpose flour
4 tablespoons margarine, room temperature
2 tablespoons reduced-fat sour cream
1 cup plus 2 tablespoons granulated sugar, divided
1 egg
2 egg whites
1 tablespoon grated lemon rind
3 tablespoons lemon juice
1/2 teaspoon baking powder
1/4 teaspoon salt
Powdered sugar, as garnish

1. Mix flour, margarine, sour cream, and 2 tablespoons granulated sugar in small bowl to form soft dough. Press dough into bottom and 1/4 inch up sides of 8-inch-square baking pan. Bake at 350° until light brown, about 20 minutes; cool on wire rack.

2. Mix remaining 1 cup granulated sugar and remaining ingredients, except powdered sugar, in small bowl; pour over baked pastry. Bake until no indentation remains when touched in the center, 20 to 25 minutes. Cool on wire rack; cut into squares. Sprinkle lightly with powdered sugar before serving.

Nutritional Data

PER COOKIE		EXCHANGES	
Calories:	72	Milk:	0.0
% Calories from fat:	28	Vegetable:	0.0
Fat (gm):	2.3	Fruit:	0.0
Sat. fat (gm):	0.6	Bread:	1.0
Cholesterol (mg):	9	Meat:	0.0
Sodium (mg):	57	Fat:	0.0
Protein (gm):	0.9		
Carbohydrate (gm):	12.2		

FROSTED COCOA BROWNIES

*Very chocolatey and slightly chewy, you'll
never guess these brownies are low in fat.*

25 Brownies

 1 cup all-purpose flour
 1 cup sugar
 1/4 cup unsweetened cocoa
 5 tablespoons margarine, melted
 1/4 cup skim milk
 1 egg
 2 egg whites
 1/4 cup honey
 1 teaspoon vanilla
    Cocoa Frosting (recipe follows)

1. Combine flour, sugar, and cocoa in medium bowl; add margarine, milk, egg, egg whites, honey, and vanilla, mixing until smooth. Pour batter into greased and floured 8-inch-square baking pan.

2. Bake at 350° until brownies spring back when touched, about 30 minutes. Cool in pan on wire rack; spread with Cocoa Frosting.

Cocoa Frosting

Makes about 1/2 cup

 1 cup powdered sugar
 2–3 tablespoons unsweetened cocoa
 1 tablespoon margarine, softened
 2–3 tablespoons skim milk

1. In small bowl, beat powdered sugar, cocoa, margarine, and enough milk to make spreading consistency.

Nutritional Data

PER BROWNIE		EXCHANGES	
Calories:	111	Milk:	0.0
% Calories from fat:	24	Vegetable:	0.0
Fat (gm):	3.1	Fruit:	1.5
Sat. fat (gm):	0.6	Bread:	0.0
Cholesterol (mg):	8.6	Meat:	0.0
Sodium (mg):	42	Fat:	0.5
Protein (gm):	1.5		
Carbohydrate (gm):	20.4		

13
PIES AND PUDDINGS

Grandma's Lemon Meringue Pie

Banana Cream Pie

Double Crust Apple Pie

Spiced Sweet Potato Pie

Angel Pie

Raisin Bread Pudding

Baked Cereal Pudding

Old-Fashioned Baked Rice Pudding

Chocolate Pudding Cake

GRANDMA'S LEMON MERINGUE PIE

A perfect flavor combination of sweet and tart, topped with a mile-high meringue! Be sure to spread the meringue while filling is hot, and seal to the edge of the crust to prevent weeping.

10 Servings

Reduced-Fat Baked Pie Crust (recipe follows)
2 cups sugar, divided
$\frac{1}{2}$ cup cornstarch
1 $\frac{1}{2}$ cups water
$\frac{1}{2}$ cup lemon juice
1 egg
2 tablespoons margarine
4 egg whites
$\frac{1}{4}$ teaspoon cream of tartar

1. Make pastry, using 9-inch pie pan. Line bottom of pastry with aluminum foil and fill with layer of pie weights or dry beans. Bake at 400° for 10 minutes; remove foil and pie weights. Continue baking until crust is golden, 5 to 8 minutes. Cool on wire rack.

2. Combine 1½ cups sugar and cornstarch in medium saucepan; stir in water and lemon juice. Heat to boiling; boil, whisking constantly, until thickened, about 1 minute.

3. Beat egg in small bowl; whisk about 1 cup of lemon mixture into egg mixture. Whisk egg mixture back into saucepan; cook over very low heat, whisking constantly, 30 to 60 seconds. Remove from heat; add margarine, stirring until melted. Pour filling into pie crust.

4. Using clean beaters and large bowl, beat egg whites until foamy; add cream of tartar and beat to soft peaks. Beat to stiff peaks, adding remaining ½ cup sugar gradually. Spread meringue over hot filling, sealing well to edge of pie crust. Bake at 400° until meringue is browned, about 5 minutes. Cool to room temperature before cutting. Refrigerate leftover pie.

Reduced-Fat Baked Pie Crust

For one 8- or 9-inch pie

1¼ cups all-purpose flour
  2 tablespoons sugar
  ¼ teaspoon salt
3–4 tablespoons vegetable shortening, *or* margarine
4–5 tablespoons ice water

1. Combine flour, sugar, and salt in medium bowl. Cut in shortening with pastry blender until mixture resembles coarse crumbs. Sprinkle with ice water, 1 tablespoon at a time, mixing with fork just until dough holds together.

2. Roll pastry on floured surface to circle 2 inches larger than inverted pie pan. Ease pastry into pan; trim and flute edge. Bake as recipe directs.

Nutritional Data

PER SERVING		EXCHANGES	
Calories:	316	Milk:	0.0
% Calories from fat:	18	Vegetable:	0.0
Fat (gm):	6.5	Fruit:	0.0
Sat. fat (gm):	1.5	Bread:	4.0
Cholesterol (mg):	21.3	Meat:	0.0
Sodium (mg):	110	Fat:	0.5
Protein (gm):	3.7		
Carbohydrate (gm):	61.6		

BANANA CREAM PIE

We've added strawberries to this old family favorite.

8 to 10 Servings

$^1\!/_3$ cup sugar
$^1\!/_4$ cup cornstarch
2 tablespoons flour
$^1\!/_8$ teaspoon salt
$2^1\!/_2$ cups skim milk
3 egg yolks
1 teaspoon vanilla
$^1\!/_4$ teaspoon ground cinnamon
$^1\!/_8$ teaspoon ground nutmeg
2 medium bananas, sliced, divided
1 cup sliced strawberries, divided
Graham Cracker Crumb Crust (recipe follows)

1. Mix sugar, cornstarch, flour, and salt in medium saucepan; stir in milk. Heat to boiling over medium-high heat, stirring constantly; boil, stirring constantly, 1 minute.

2. Whisk about 1 cup milk mixture into egg yolks in small bowl; whisk egg mixture back into saucepan. Cook over very low heat, stirring constantly, 30 to 60 seconds. Remove from heat; stir in vanilla and spices. Cool to room temperature, stirring frequently.

3. Arrange $^3\!/_4$ of sliced bananas and $^3\!/_4$ cup strawberries in bottom of baked Crumb Crust. Spoon custard evenly over top. Refrigerate until custard is set, 6 to 8 hours. Before serving, garnish top of pie with remaining bananas and strawberries.

Graham Cracker Crumb Crust

$1^1\!/_2$ cups graham cracker crumbs
3 tablespoons margarine, melted
1–2 tablespoons honey

1. Combine graham crumbs, margarine, and honey in bottom of 9-inch pie pan; pat mixture evenly on bottom and side of pan. Bake at 350° until lightly browned, 8 to 10 minutes. Cool on wire rack.

Variation

Coconut Cream Pie: Delete bananas and strawberries in above recipe. Stir $^1\!/_4$ cup toasted coconut into cooked custard. Sprinkle top of pie with 1 to 2 tablespoons toasted coconut.

Nutritional Data

PER SERVING		EXCHANGES	
Calories:	281	Milk:	0.0
% Calories from fat:	29	Vegetable:	0.0
Fat (gm):	9.2	Fruit:	1.0
Sat. fat (gm):	1.6	Bread:	2.0
Cholesterol (mg):	81.1	Meat:	0.0
Sodium (mg):	244	Fat:	1.5
Protein (gm):	5.8		
Carbohydrate (gm):	44.7		

DOUBLE CRUST APPLE PIE

Nothing is more American than real homemade apple pie. Enjoy this one warm with a generous scoop of fat-free frozen yogurt or a slice of reduced-fat Cheddar cheese.

10 Servings

Double-Crust Pastry (recipe follows)
8 cups peeled, cored, sliced tart baking apples
1 cup sugar
4–5 tablespoons all-purpose flour
3/4 teaspoon ground cinnamon
1/4 teaspoon ground nutmeg
1/8 teaspoon ground cloves
1/8 teaspoon salt
2 tablespoons margarine, cut into pieces (optional)

1. Roll 2/3 of pastry on floured surface to form circle 2 inches larger than inverted 9-inch pie pan; ease pastry into pan.

2. Toss apples with combined sugar, flour, spices, and salt in large bowl; arrange apples in pastry shell and dot with margarine.

3. Roll remaining pastry to fit top of pie and place over apples. Trim edges of pastry to within 1/2 inch of pan; fold top pastry over bottom pastry and flute. Cut vents in top crust.

4. Bake pie at 425° until apples are fork-tender and pastry browned, 40 to 50 minutes. Cover pastry with aluminum foil if it is becoming too brown. Cool 10 to 15 minutes before cutting.

Double-Crust Pastry

Makes double crust for 8- or 9-inch pie

2 cups all-purpose flour
3 tablespoons sugar
½ teaspoon salt
5 tablespoons cold margarine, cut into pieces
6–7 tablespoons ice water

1. Combine flour, sugar, and salt in medium bowl; cut in margarine with pastry blender until mixture resembles coarse crumbs. Add water, a tablespoon at a time, mixing with fork, until dough forms. Refrigerate until ready to use.

Nutritional Data

PER SERVING		EXCHANGES	
Calories:	297	Milk:	0.0
% Calories from fat:	19	Vegetable:	0.0
Fat (gm):	6.3	Fruit:	1.0
Sat. fat (gm):	1.2	Bread:	3.5
Cholesterol (mg):	0	Meat:	0.0
Sodium (mg):	200	Fat:	1.5
Protein (gm):	3.1		
Carbohydrate (gm):	58.9		

SPICED SWEET POTATO PIE

Down-home and simply delicious! Substitute canned pumpkin for the sweet potatoes if you like.

8 to 10 Servings

Reduced-Fat Pie Crust (see p. 139)
1½ cups mashed sweet potatoes
¾ cup packed light brown sugar
1 egg
2 egg whites
1½ cups skim milk
1 teaspoon ground cinnamon
1 teaspoon ground ginger
½ teaspoon ground mace
¼ teaspoon salt
Light whipped topping (optional)

1. Make Pie Pastry, adding 2 tablespoons of sugar to the flour mixture. Roll pastry on floured surface to form circle 2 inches larger than inverted 8-inch pie pan. Ease pastry into pan, trim, and flute.

2. Mix sweet potatoes, brown sugar, egg, egg whites, milk, spices, and salt in large bowl until smooth. Pour mixture into pastry shell.

3. Bake at 350° until filling is set and sharp knife inserted near center comes out clean, about 45 minutes. Serve warm or at room temperature; garnish with whipped topping.

Variation

Spiced Pumpkin Pie: Substitute 1½ cups canned pumpkin for the sweet potatoes.

Nutritional Data

PER SERVING		EXCHANGES	
Calories:	295	Milk:	0.0
% Calories from fat:	16	Vegetable:	0.0
Fat (gm):	5.4	Fruit:	0.0
Sat. fat (gm):	1.2	Bread:	3.5
Cholesterol (mg):	27.4	Meat:	0.0
Sodium (mg):	245	Fat:	1.0
Protein (gm):	6.3		
Carbohydrate (gm):	55.9		

ANGEL PIE

◆

As heavenly as its name, this pie will tempt second servings!

8 Servings

1½ cups frozen light whipped topping, thawed
1½ cups low-fat custard-style lemon yogurt
2 tablespoons grated lemon rind
   Meringue Pie Shell (recipe follows)
   Lemon slices, as garnish
   Mint sprigs, as garnish

1. Mix whipped topping, yogurt, and lemon rind in small bowl; spoon into baked Meringue Pie Shell. Refrigerate until serving time.

2. Garnish pie with lemon slices and mint; cut into wedges.

Note

Any desired flavor of low-fat custard-style yogurt can be substituted for lemon.

Meringue Pie Shell

4 egg whites
⅛ teaspoon cream of tartar
1 cup sugar

1. Beat egg whites in large bowl until foamy; beat in cream of tartar and beat to soft peaks. Continue beating to stiff peaks, adding sugar gradually.

2. Spoon mixture into ungreased 9-inch pie pan, spreading on bottom and up side to form a large bowl shape. Bake at 300° until lightly browned and firm to touch, about 40 minutes. Turn heat off but let shell remain in oven 1 hour. Cool on wire rack.

Nutritional Data

PER SERVING		EXCHANGES	
Calories:	170	Milk:	0.5
% Calories from fat:	12	Vegetable:	0.0
Fat (gm):	2.3	Fruit:	0.0
Sat. fat (gm):	1.8	Bread:	1.5
Cholesterol (mg):	2.6	Meat:	0.0
Sodium (mg):	57	Fat:	0.5
Protein (gm):	3.5		
Carbohydrate (gm):	34.8		

RAISIN BREAD PUDDING

*For the best pudding, use a firm-textured
bread that is day-old or slightly stale.*

6 to 8 Servings

6-8 slices white, *or* wholewheat bread
3 tablespoons margarine, softened
1/3 cup raisins
1 egg
2 egg whites
1/2 cup sugar
1/4 teaspoon salt
2 cups skim milk
1 teaspoon vanilla

1. Spread 1 side of bread slices with margarine; cut into 1-inch squares (about 6 cups). Combine bread cubes and raisins in greased 1½-quart casserole.

2. Mix egg, egg whites, sugar, and salt in medium bowl. Heat milk and vanilla to simmering in small saucepan; whisk into egg mixture. Pour over bread cubes and toss to moisten.

3. Place casserole in roasting pan on oven rack; pour 2 inches hot water into pan. Bake, uncovered, at 350° until pudding is set and sharp knife inserted near center comes out clean, 35 to 40 minutes. Serve warm or at room temperature.

Nutritional Data

PER SERVING		EXCHANGES	
Calories:	250	Milk:	0.0
% Calories from fat:	27	Vegetable:	0.0
Fat (gm):	7.6	Fruit:	0.5
Sat. fat (gm):	1.7	Bread:	2.0
Cholesterol (mg):	36.8	Meat:	0.0
Sodium (mg):	345	Fat:	1.5
Protein (gm):	7.2		
Carbohydrate (gm):	38.7		

BAKED CEREAL PUDDING

Eat warm from the oven, or refrigerate for a chilled dessert. Either way, this comfort food is just delicious.

6 Servings (¹/₂ cup each)

    2 eggs
    2 egg whites
    ¹/₄ cup sugar
    ¹/₄ cup packed brown sugar
    ³/₄ cup natural wheat and barley cereal
         (Grape-Nuts)
    2 cups skim milk
    2 tablespoons margarine, melted
    1 teaspoon vanilla
    ¹/₈ teaspoon salt

1. Beat eggs, egg whites, and sugars in medium bowl; mix in remaining ingredients.

2. Pour mixture into 1-quart soufflé dish or casserole. Place dish in roasting pan on oven rack; pour 2 inches hot water into pan. Bake, uncovered, at 375° until pudding is set, about 50 minutes, stirring well halfway through baking time.

3. Remove soufflé dish from pan; cool on wire rack. Serve warm, or refrigerate and serve chilled.

Nutritional Data

PER SERVING		EXCHANGES	
Calories:	214	Milk:	0.0
% Calories from fat:	24	Vegetable:	0.0
Fat (gm):	5.8	Fruit:	0.0
Sat. fat (gm):	1.4	Bread:	2.0
Cholesterol (mg):	72.3	Meat:	0.5
Sodium (mg):	262	Fat:	1.0
Protein (gm):	7.9		
Carbohydrate (gm):	33.2		

OLD-FASHIONED BAKED RICE PUDDING

*This nourishing dessert is best served
warm and fresh from the oven.*

4 to 6 Servings

$1/2$ cup uncooked converted rice

3 cups skim milk

$1/3$ cup sugar

$1/4$ cup raisins

$1/2$ teaspoon ground cinnamon

2 dashes ground nutmeg

1. Combine rice, milk, sugar, raisins, cinnamon, and nutmeg in 2-quart casserole. Bake, uncovered, at 350° until rice is tender and milk is absorbed, about $2^1/2$ hours, stirring occasionally.

Nutritional Data

PER SERVING		EXCHANGES	
Calories:	243	Milk:	1.0
% Calories from fat:	2	Vegetable:	0.0
Fat (gm):	0.5	Fruit:	0.5
Sat. fat (gm):	0	Bread:	2.0
Cholesterol (mg):	3	Meat:	0.0
Sodium (mg):	97	Fat:	0.0
Protein (gm):	8.1		
Carbohydrate (gm):	51.9		

CHOCOLATE PUDDING CAKE

The ultimate comfort food, this dessert bakes into a luscious combination of pudding and cake! Serve warm with a spoonful of fat-free ice cream or light whipped topping.

4 Servings

$^{1}/_{2}$ cup all-purpose flour
$^{1}/_{4}$ cup granulated sugar
4 tablespoons unsweetened cocoa, divided
$^{3}/_{4}$ teaspoon baking powder
$^{1}/_{8}$ teaspoon salt
$^{1}/_{4}$ cup skim milk
2 tablespoons margarine, melted
$^{1}/_{2}$ teaspoon vanilla
$^{1}/_{2}$ cup packed light brown sugar
$^{2}/_{3}$ cup boiling water
$^{1}/_{4}$ cup coarsely chopped walnuts

1. Mix flour, granulated sugar, 2 tablespoons cocoa, baking powder, salt, milk, margarine, and vanilla in 1-quart casserole until smooth.

2. Add brown sugar and remaining 2 tablespoons cocoa to boiling water in 2-cup glass measure, stirring until sugar is dissolved. Pour mixture over batter in casserole; sprinkle with walnuts.

3. Bake, uncovered, at 350° until toothpick inserted in cake comes out clean, about 30 minutes. Serve warm in bowls.

Nutritional Data

PER SERVING		EXCHANGES	
Calories:	325	Milk:	0.0
% Calories from fat:	28	Vegetable:	0.0
Fat (gm):	10.8	Fruit:	0.0
Sat. fat (gm):	1.6	Bread:	3.5
Cholesterol (mg):	0.3	Meat:	0.0
Sodium (mg):	217	Fat:	1.5
Protein (gm):	5.1		
Carbohydrate (gm):	56.3		

INDEX

A

Angel Pie, 144
Apple-Date Filling, 116
Apple Pie, Double Crust, 141
Artichokes with Hollandaise
    Sauce, 72

B

Banana Bread, 111
Banana Cream Pie, 140
Barley, Beef, and Vegetable Soup, 10
Beans, Baked, New England, 74
Bean, Green, Casserole, 73
Bean, Navy, Soup with Ham, 9
Beef, Barley, and Vegetable Soup, 10
Beef Bourguignonne, 19
Beef Stew, Country, 21
Beef Stroganoff, 20
Beets, Harvard, 75
Biscuits, Vinegar, 107
Boston Cream Pie, 127
BREADS, 105-113
Bread Pudding, Raisin, 145
Brownies, Cocoa, Frosted, 136
Bubble Loaf, 108
Buns, Sticky, 112

C

Cacciatore, Chicken, 38
Caesar Salad, 97
CAKES, 115-130
Cake, Chocolate Pudding, 148
Carrot Cake with Cream Cheese
    Frosting, 123
Carrot-Raisin Salad, 90
Cauliflower with Creamy Cheese
    Sauce, 76
Cereal Pudding, Baked, 146

Cheese, Cheddar, Soufflé, 68
Cheese Fondue, 69
Cheese Sauce, Creamy, 76
Cheeseburgers Supreme, 101
Chicken
    Cacciatore, 38
    Cordon Bleu, 34
    Crisp Oven-Fried, 32
    Fricassee, 41
    à la King in Toast Cups, 35
    Legs, Mock, 27
    Paprikash, 37
    Roast, with Cornbread Stuffing, 33
    Stew, with Parsley Dumplings, 39
Chicken-Fried Steak, 16
Chicken Noodle Soup, 4
Chili con Carne, 7
Chili Mac, 8
Chocolate Buttermilk Cake with
    Mocha Frosting, 121
Chocolate Chip Cookies, 132
Chocolate Glaze, 128
Chocolate Pudding Cake, 148
Chop Suey, 28
Chowder, New England Clam, 6
Chowder, Potato, 5
Cinnamon Rolls, 113
Clam Chowder, New England, 6
Clam Sauce, White, with
    Linguini, 60
Cocoa Brownies, Frosted, 136
Cocoa Frosting, 136
Coconut Cream Pie, 140
Coffee Cake, Sour Cream, with
    Apple-Date Filling, 116
Coleslaw (Perfection Salad), 88
Coleslaw, Freezer, 94
COOKIES, 131-136
Corn Pudding, 77
Cornish Hens, Glazed, with Wild
    Rice, 42

Crab Melt, 102
Cream Cheese Glaze, 117
Cream of Mushroom Soup, 3
Cream of Tomato Soup, 2
Crumb Crust, Graham
    Cracker, 140
Crust, Pie
  Double-Crust Pastry, 142
  Graham Cracker Crumb, 140
  for Meringue Pie, 144
  Reduced-Fat Baked, 139

D

Dressing, Herbed Sour Cream, 98
Dumplings, Parsley, 40

E

Eggs Benedict, 64
English Muffin Bread, 109

F

Filling
  Apple-Date, 116
  Vanilla Cream, 128
FISH, 47-54
Flounder en Papillote, 51
French Fries, 82
French Toast, 110
Fricassee, Chicken, 41
Frosting
  Cocoa, 136
  Cream Cheese, 123
  Mocha, 122
  Penuche, 125
  Sugar, 134
Fruit Salad, Frozen, 89

G

Garlic Bread, 106
Glaze, Chocolate, 128
Glaze, Cream Cheese, 117
Graham Cracker Crumb Crust, 140
Gravy, Cream, 25
Gravy, Mushroom, 24
Green Bean Casserole, 73

H

Ham à la King, 36
Harvard Beets, 75
Hash
  Corned Beef, 26
  Mexican, 27
  Roast Beef, 26
Hollandaise Sauce, Mock, 64

I

Ice Cream Jelly Roll Cake, 129

J

Jelly Roll Cake, Ice Cream,
    129, 130

L

Lasagne, Italian, 61
Lemon Meringue Pie,
    Grandma's, 138
Lemon Pound Cake, 119
Lemon Squares, Tart, 135
Lemon Syrup, 120
Linguini with White Clam
    Sauce, 60

M

Macaroni and Cheese, 56
Macaroni and Cheese
    Primavera, 56
Macaroni Salad, 93
Mashed Potatoes, Real, 78
MEATS, 13-30
Meat Loaf, Just Plain, 22
Meatballs, 59
Meatballs, Swedish, with
    Noodles, 25
Meringue Pie, Grandma's
    Lemon, 138
Meringue Pie Shell, 144
Mocha Frosting, 122
Mock Chicken Legs, 27
Monte Cristo, 103
Mushroom Gravy, 24
Mushroom Soup, Cream of, 3

N

Navy Bean Soup with Ham, 9
New England Baked Beans, 74
New England Clam Chowder, 6
Newburg, Seafood, 53
Nutritional data, xiii (*see also* with
   individual recipes)

O

Oatmeal Raisin Cookies, 133
Orange Chiffon Cake, Glazed, 118

P

Pancakes, Potato, 78
Paprikash, Chicken, 37
PASTA, 55-62
Pastry, Pie, 66 (*see also* Pie Crust)
Pea Sauce, Creamed, 48
Pea, Split, Soup with Ham, 11
Penuche Frosting, 125
Pepper Steak, 15
Pepper Steak, Sweet-Sour, 16
Peppers, Stuffed Green, 23
PIES, 138-144
Pie Crust
   Double-Crust Pastry, 142
   Graham Cracker Crumb, 140
   for Meringue Pie, 144
   Reduced-Fat Baked, 139
Pie Pastry, Reduced-Fat, 66
Poppy Seed Pound Cake,
   Lemon, 120
Pork Chops with Bread
   Stuffing, 34
Pot Pie Pastry, 45
Pot Pie, Turkey, 44
Pot Roast, Old-Fashioned, 17
Potatoes
   Baked Sloppy, 100
   Baked (Twice) with Cheese, 81
   Fries, Crispy, 82
   Gratin, 79
   Mashed, 78
   Parmesan Fries, 82
   Scalloped, 80
   Steak Fries, 82
Potato Chowder, 5

Potato Pancakes, 78
Potato Salad, Creamy, 91
Potato Salad, German, 92
POULTRY, 31-45
Pound Cake, Lemon, 119
Pound Cake, Poppy Seed, 120
PUDDINGS, 145-148
Pumpkin Pie, Spiced, 143

Q

Quiche Lorraine, 65
Quiche, Spinach, 66

R

Raisin Bread, 109
Raisin Bread Pudding, 145
Raisin Oatmeal Cookies, 133
Rarebit, Welsh, 67
Rice Pudding, Old-Fashioned
   Baked, 147
Rolls, Cinnamon, 113

S

SALADS, 87-98
Salisbury Steak with Mushroom
   Gravy, 23
Salmon, Poached, with Hollandaise
   Sauce, 50
SANDWICHES, 99-103
Sauces
   Cheese, Creamy, 76
   Clam, White, 60
   Hollandaise, Mock, 64
   Pea, Creamed, 48
   Tomato, Herbed, 61
Scalloped Potatoes, 80
   and Ham, 80
Seafood Newburg, 53
Shell, Pie, 144
Shepherd's Pie, 29
Shrimp De Jonghe, 52
Sloppy Joes, 100
Soufflé, Cheddar Cheese, 68
SOUPS, 1-11
Spaghetti and Meatballs, 58
Spice Cake with Penuche
   Frosting, 124

Spinach, Creamed, 83
Spinach Quiche, 66
Spinach Salad, Wilted, 96
Split Pea Soup with Ham, 11
Steak
  Chicken-Fried, 16
  Pepper, 15
  au Poivre, 14
  Salisbury, with Mushroom
    Gravy, 23
  Sweet-Sour Pepper, 16
Stew
  Beef Bourguignonne, 19
  Beef, Country, 21
  Chicken, with Parsley
    Dumplings, 39
Sticky Buns, 112
Stroganoff, Beef, 20
Stuffed Green Peppers, 23
Sugar Cookies, Frosted, 134
Swedish Meatballs with Noodles, 25
Sweet Potato Pie, Spiced, 143
Syrup, Lemon, 120

T

Ten-Layer Salad, 98
Tetrazzini, Turkey, 57
Toast Cups, 36

Tomato Pudding, 84
Tomato Sauce, Herbed, 61
Tomato Soup, Cream of, 2
Tuna Patties with Creamed Pea
    Sauce, 48
Turkey
  Divan, 43
  Pot Pie, 44
  Tetrazzini, 57

U

Upside-Down Cake, Pineapple, 126

V

Vanilla Cream Filling, 128
VEGETABLES, 71-86
Vegetable Soup, Beef, Barley
    and, 10
Vichyssoise, 5

W

Waldorf Salad, 95
Welsh Rarebit, 67

Y

Yams, Candied, 86